Ensuring Fairness in Health Care Coverage

An Employer's Guide to Making Good Decisions on Tough Issues

Matthew K. Wynia and
Abraham P. Schwab

AMACOM

American Management Association

New York • Atlanta • Brussels • Chicago • Mexico City • San Francisco
Shanghai • Tokyo • Toronto • Washington, D.C.

This publication is designed to provide accurate and authoritative
information in regard to the subject matter covered. It is sold with
the understanding that the publisher is not engaged in rendering
legal, accounting, or other professional service. If legal advice or
other expert assistance is required, the services of a competent
professional person should be sought.

With the exception of case 1 in Chapter 5, all cases presented in this
book have been fictionalized. Business and individual names are
fictional. Any resemblance to actual organizations or persons, living
or deceased, is purely coincidental.

The views and opinions in this book are those of the authors and
should not be construed as policy positions either of the American
Medical Association or the other organizations involved in the
Ethical Force Program.

Library of Congress Cataloging-in-Publication Data

Wynia, Matthew K.
        Ensuring fairness in health care coverage : an employer's guide to making
good decisions on tough issues / Matthew K. Wynia and Abraham P. Schwab.
        p.   cm.
    Includes index.
    ISBN-13: 978-0-8144-7384-9
    ISBN-10: 0-8144-7384-9
    1. Employer-sponsored health insurance—United States.   2. Insurance,
Health—United States.   I. Schwab, Abraham P.   II. Title.

HG9396.W96   2007
658.3'254—dc22   2006024193

Printing number

10   9   8   7   6   5   4   3   2   1

Contents

Foreword

It is fashionable just now to believe that health care coverage, health care costs, and health itself should be driven by consumer choice and are the individual's responsibility. Yet business knows that coverage in health care is a collective enterprise, so that individuals act within an organizational context. Though we may sometimes wish to deny it, both general and specific issues of health and health care costs are often our joint responsibility. We act with compassion in ensuring that children are vaccinated against measles. But we also act in the knowledge that we will be protected from measles if almost all are vaccinated. In a market driven, quarterly profit driven world, these kinds of long term interventions can seem only impediments to business success. It is reasonable to imagine that they are impediments to successful competition only in the short term and that long-term success means acknowledging that ethical processes support the business directly.

Ethics in business and ethics in health care are related. Nowhere is this more obvious than in the design and development of health care insurance coverage. To be compassionate, fair, transparent, consistent, participatory, and sensitive to value is to follow guides that build the workforce. Health care businesses do not always model ethical values in an unambiguous fashion. The integrity of biomedical research is questioned. Product flaws are hidden. Government actions are quixotic. Even direct patient care by physicians does not always model the central values of transparency. Patients may not be told what their options are or may undergo unnecessary tests that support the physician or his organization.

For these reasons we often turn to the legal system or to government or non-governmental regulators to "enforce" certain standards of conduct and to report violations. The unfortunate side effect of relying on the external enforcement of standards is that it reinforces the idea that ethical business behavior interferes with the pursuit of market success. Regulation and its inspection based process require resources that can seem to divert attention from an organization's central goals, whether they be market share, profit, or some other important metric. Even more legal and other resources can be required if a business seeks to uncover loopholes in the legal or regulatory process. Reliance on external review of business behavior can thereby divert attention from the positive contributions to success that can follow from affirmative ethical behavior.

Health care costs can seem to be a major cost for a business pursuing success. This means that the design of health insurance coverage is an important exemplar. Health care itself can certainly contribute to business success by improving the productivity of the workforce. In fact, some of the earliest and most convincing studies of the positive effects of alcoholism programs, depression screening, workplace safety standards, etc., were centered on the workplace and quantified in terms that relate to the success of businesses in the marketplace.

More elusive is the problem of whether ethical behaviors can make a general contribution to business success. To argue that such behavior does make a difference relies on soft concerns that are difficult to quantify and sometimes long-term in nature. There is not much question that building a confident, dedicated workforce that feels engaged with the business is of positive value. Even though a "satisfied" workforce is rarely an appropriate goal, *engaged* employees are a positive force. Similarly, building trust among customers and suppliers has long-term positive effects on success.

To support the sense of the positive contribution of ethical behavior, one most often looks at the failures. Inability to trust the company's accounting process has led to precipitous failures. Inability to trust a pharmaceutical company's reported research can destroy the credibility of its products. But business success, in whatever terms, is not simply the absence of failure.

As the classic work of Lynn Paine[1] has underscored, it is possible to build a successful business by complying with externally composed and imposed rules. But it is more effective to build a business with an internally consistent "integrity structure." Such a business depends on many of the principles that have been examined in *Ensuring Fairness in Health Care Coverage*.

So, ethical business is not an oxymoron. In fact, ethical action is the foundation of both individual business success and of the success of the market environment in which we live. Without attention to values and to their inevitable conflicts, we have no structure within which to act. Fairness in health care coverage is part of that ethical structure.

John M. Ludden, MD, FACPE
Norman S. Stearns MD Professor of Health Management
Department of Public Health and Family Medicine
Tufts University Medical School

[1] Paine, Lynn Sharp, "Managing for Organizational Integrity," Harvard Business Review, March–April 1994, pp. 107–117.

Acknowledgments

No book reflects the work of its author or authors alone. This book provides an extreme example of this fact. The present work stems directly from the work of the Ethical Force Program and its oversight body, as well as an appointed expert advisory panel on benefits determinations (see appendix A). The process of developing consensus on an ethical framework for making coverage decisions was contentious, raucous, stimulating, and, ultimately, very rewarding. In retrospect, it was probably a risky task—bringing together stakeholders as diverse as health plans, employers, unions, doctors, nurses, and patient groups to discuss, in essence, how to ration health care ethically. And yet, in the end, this group of smart and dedicated people came together and recognized some core shared values. The authors can take only modest credit for the success of this foundational work.

Next, following publication of the Ethical Force Program's consensus report, Renee Witlen, then a fellow in the American Medical Association's Institute for Ethics, was charged with doing research on how the consensus report might provide guidance in actual purchasing situations. It was Renee who began the arduous process of conducting interviews, sending e-mails, scouring the Web and newspaper stories, and much of the other research that ultimately found its way into the many examples used in the book. Renee also first approached publishers with the possibility of formulating this research into a book, and she wrote an initial model chapter before she headed off to New York to prepare for medical school last year. In sum, if the Ethical Force Program gave birth to the idea for this book, Renee raised the infant into a robust childhood. Renee is brilliant. And if this book is helpful, it is because of the groundwork that she laid. It came as no surprise to us when she received multiple medical school acceptance letters this year.

Among the many members of the Ethical Force Program's oversight body, several deserve special mention for their help in developing this book. Russell Teagarden, Inger Saphire-Bernstein, Michael J. Fitzmaurice, David Fleming, and Ed Martinez each provided timely, substantive, and constructive comments on a number of chapters.

Appendix B is a concise summary of a longer report by Melane Kinney Hoffman and George I. Balch as well as one of the current authors (MKW). They organized and ran the focus groups, which were funded in part by the U.S. Agency for Health Care Research and Quality. To fit it into the appendix, we cut the report by more than half of its original length—any errors or lack of clarity that resulted from this editing process are the sole responsibility of the present authors.

The process of doing research and developing and disseminating the consensus report would not have been possible without financial support from a number of sources. We received grants for this initiative from the American Nurses Association, the David and Carolyn Fleming Charitable Foundation, GlaxoSmith-Kline, the Joint Commission on Accreditation of Healthcare Organizations, the National Health Council, and the Parkland Health and Hospital System.

We also wish to acknowledge the support of our editor at AMACOM, Adrienne Hickey, and the assistance of our copy editor, Douglas Puchowski. Adrienne was firm yet kind when we missed an early deadline, and she was creative and flexible when it was needed most. Douglas helped to clarify and refine a number of key passages, probably saving us considerable embarrassment in the process. Any errors of grammar or meaning that remain are probably things we insisted on retaining despite his advice to the contrary.

Among organizations, the American Medical Association deserves very special credit. The AMA has provided untold support, financial and otherwise, to the work of the Ethical Force Program from Day 1—despite potential controversy, and, we must note, with little realistic hope of any significant monetary return on this investment. The American Medical Association's steadfast commitment to ethics in health care is what makes it possible for the Institute for Ethics to exist—and therefore for both of us to do what we love.

Which brings us to our personal thanks, because we also would not have been able to write this book without the support and help of those we love.

MKW: I would like to extend special thanks to several colleagues at the AMA—Audiey Kao, MD, PhD, Karine Morin, LLM, and Faith Lagay, PhD are my key professional sounding boards, but more importantly they are good friends. And without Jeanne Uehling and Jennifer Matiasek, the work of the Institute for Ethics would quite likely grind to a halt. They are invaluable to me. Finally, over the last twenty years I have spent countless happy hours with my wife, Romana Hasnain-Wynia, PhD, talking about health care, ethics, and why all of this really matters. She has the uncanny ability to keep me grounded, while lifting my heart to the stars. Our amazing children, Kavon, Aiden, and Zan, are reminders of the precious gift of health—and of just how lucky we are.

APS: Along with Matt, I would also like to thank my AMA colleagues. Faith Lagay and Karine Morin have been mentors to me, each in their own way, and Audiey Kao has been a constant challenge to my presumptions about the ethics of health care. I would also like to thank Matt for the opportunity to work on this book and for his leadership through the writing and publishing process. For her companionship, encouragement and advice, I cannot thank my wife, Liz, enough. Drawing from her experience as a professional writer and editor, she gave my ideas legs. Finally, our infant son Daniel, with his constant smile and giddy laugh, reminds me how easy it is to be happy when you're healthy.

The Issues and Principles of Fair Health Care Decisions

What's Fair?

An Introduction to Fairness Issues

*I*n response to a number of employee requests, FitWell, a regional clothing retailer with about 200 employees, is changing
health plans. Employees want a health plan with lower premiums.
After a good deal of work negotiating and conversing with several
national insurance companies and her broker, Anna Mueller, Fit-
Well's owner, has designed an HMO plan that seems to meet with
general support from most of her employees.

Some employees, however, have expressed reservations about
the plan's restrictions on in-network physicians. One employee in
particular, Aaron Dufresne, expresses his concern more vehe-
mently. But while Aaron is a valued employee who has been with
the company for almost ten years, the few other employees who
have mentioned concerns about the in-network physicians have
nevertheless endorsed the change. It seems most employees are
pleased with the new plan.

In the weeks after the decision to change plans, Aaron approaches Anna and explains the reasons for his reservations. He
has recently been diagnosed as HIV-positive and feels he needs
to continue his relationship with his primary care physician. The
relationship goes back twenty years, so he is very worried about

switching to a new physician. Will he even be able to find one he likes and who will really get to know him like his current doctor does?

Anna listens to his frustrations, and after he has finished, she expresses sympathy for his position, but, she explains, she has to focus on the best plan for her entire group of employees. Although she understands his worries and his special sense of vulnerability in changing to a new doctor, she also emphasizes that the decision about the health plan has already been made. The contract for the new plan has been signed.

Aaron says, "If I can't go back to my doc through my insurance here, I'm going to have to look for another job where I can. You know I don't want to leave. I've been here so long, and I love these people and this company, but I really need to know that I can trust my doctor. Isn't there anything you can do?"

What course of action do you think would be the most fair response to Aaron's request? Perhaps fairness requires Anna to draw a line in the sand and tell Aaron that it's unfortunate, but the decision has been made and there is no going back. Or does fairness require Anna to make an exception for Aaron? Should she make an exception because of Aaron's especially vulnerable position? Or would making an exception be unfair to her other employees? Should it matter to Anna that Aaron is a valuable employee? Should Anna decide whether to allow an exception for Aaron based on his status in the company? How productive is he? How easily could she find someone to replace him? What is the quality of his work? What if he were the head of her retail sales team? Should these issues make a difference in her decision?

The book you are holding is designed to help you grapple with questions like these. It is a casebook, designed to help you identify and respond to these ethical and practical dilemmas. We aren't going to tell you what you "must" do in a case like Aaron's—we aren't the health coverage police—but we will try to help you think and communicate clearly to your employees about what is required for your decisions about health coverage to be fair.

This is no small task. Health care coverage decisions can be the most vexing decisions made in small, medium, and even large businesses. Whether you are the human resources manager of a large corporation or the owner of a small business, choosing health care coverage can be a challenge. Anyone who has been on the receiving end of an employee complaint about their health plan—and almost everyone who has been involved in making these decisions has been—will know how wrenching these conversations can be. Making sure that coverage decisions are fair, and being able to explain this to employees, demands skills and knowledge that are rarely taught in business schools.

Foundations

The Ethical Force Program (more about this at the end of the chapter) has been working for the last two years to develop ways to help decision-makers like you in these situations.

In preparing this book, the program started out by carrying out extensive consultations, over more than a year, with a national expert advisory panel on health care benefits decisions (the names of the individuals on this panel are in appendix A). At the same time, it also conducted a series of focus groups with small, medium, and large employers (the results of these focus groups are summarized in appendix B). Through these focus groups and discussions, the program learned that insurance brokers and human resources consultants play a critical role in providing employers with information about health insurance options. So the program conducted a set of focus groups with insurance brokers and human resources consultants who specialize in health care issues (which are also summarized in appendix B). After this, the program undertook an extensive effort to call employer groups, individual employers, and others to better understand current approaches to employer-based health coverage decision-making—what works, what doesn't, and why.

To summarize these efforts, we developed a consensus report in 2003, which we called *Ensuring Fairness in Health Care Coverage Decisions*. This report, written as an academic treatise, presented an ethical framework for designing and administering health benefits, including five key ethical principles for making fair health care coverage decisions (see exhibit 1-1). It also provided a set of almost fifty specific, measurable actions that businesses could take if they wanted to emulate the best practices we had learned about and establish the most fair decision-making processes we could envision.

The report was published in an ethics journal, *The American Journal of Bioethics*, and it received a good deal of attention from ethicists. That's good, we thought. But then again, ethicists often spend their lives thinking about what is "fair" and what is not. On the downside, the report seemed not to have attracted much attention among businesses, for whom we thought it would be most useful.

EXHIBIT 1-1
THE FIVE ETHICAL GUIDEPOSTS
FOR MAKING FAIR HEALTH CARE
COVERAGE DECISIONS

All coverage decisions should be:

—Transparent

—Participatory

—Consistent

—Sensitive to Value, and

—Compassionate

We should have known better. After all, the report was not written for benefits managers, company presidents, or insurance brokers, even though their experiences had informed the creation of the report and they make most decisions about how to design health plans for their employees. Instead, it was written as an academic research paper on organizational ethics.

Most notably, the consensus report didn't have any examples of how to apply the principles. That left some of our business colleagues and friends who read the paper wondering, "How can I actually use this report to make better benefits decisions?"

That is the reason this book was written: To translate the information in the Ethical Force Program's consensus report on *Ensuring Fairness in Health Care Coverage Decisions* into meaningful examples and possible actions for you. Because, if you are reading this, you are probably involved in actually designing health care benefits for a group of employees. And you know the troubles that can arise when employees think that health coverage decisions are not fair.

Audience

If you make decisions about health care coverage for yourself and your employees, this book is for you. Any business, from a small start-up to a multinational Fortune 500 company, should try to make ethically defensible health care coverage decisions—which means they need to be fair. In different businesses these coverage decisions will often be different, depending on the scale of operations, available resources, and so on. But making good decisions about health coverage has similar advantages for any business. And the key ethical principles for making fair decisions, which we will call "Ethical Guideposts" in this book, are always the same.

The director of a large human resources department will reap the same benefits from being transparent and encouraging employee participation as the owner of a small Web design firm will. Both might need to look to outside experts to evaluate the quality of different competing health plans and to ensure their decisions are sensitive to value. Both are likely to struggle with the tension between being compassionate and flexible while also being equitable and consistent when making tough health care coverage decisions. In other words, no matter what size business you are involved with, if you have to make decisions about health care coverage, this book will help you make them fairly.

Form and Function

Each one of the book's chapters begins with a difficult health coverage case for a small, medium, or large business. Like the case that started this introduction, these cases set the stage for the chapter that follows. Each chapter is designed to explain how to follow one Ethical Guidepost when making health care coverage decisions—using real-world terms and real-world situations. Most of these cases are true stories that we have collected over the last two years. Of course, the names and certain details have been changed—after all, we don't intend to embarrass anyone—but the general stories represent real situations. In many cases, in fact, the stories are composites. We heard similar stories over and over, and often we have combined the features of more than one company's experience in the case examples.

Following the opening case, each chapter will have a brief explanation of the main focus of the chapter. Since the core of the book is the five chapters that are organized around the Five Ethical Guideposts, in each of these chapters we'll talk about the most likely concerns when applying each Ethical Guidepost in important business contexts.

Then we'll close each chapter with some more real-life cases and discussion. These additional cases will help to explain in more detail how to apply the Ethical Guidepost in certain especially tough situations. By the end of each chapter, we hope you will have a clear idea about the Ethical Guidepost we discussed as well as some specific ideas about what it could mean for your business's future health care coverage decisions.

The Stages of Health Care Coverage Decisions

There are at least three stages of health care coverage decisions for most employers. We'll call these Access, Design, and Administration.

Access to Insurance

The first decision that might come to mind is the decision about whether or not to offer any type of health insurance at all. We will take it as a given that if you bought this book, you have already decided that offering some kind of health insurance is the right thing to do for your employees and your business. But even though that is an ethically commendable decision, and probably business-savvy as well, it's just the beginning. Once you decide that you ought to offer health insurance, a large range of options opens up. That's what we're mainly going to talk about in this book. How do you make choices from among the many options available so that you are as fair as possible, and therefore least likely to run into problems over the long run?

Designing a Health Benefits Package

Designing a health care benefits package means making decisions about what sorts of things will be covered (for example, will eyeglasses, specific prescription drugs, certain screening tests, or experimental treatments be covered?) and under what general circumstances. It includes consideration of what form of health insurance plan(s) to offer (such as preferred provider organizations, health maintenance organizations, indemnity plans, and so on), and what co-payments, deductibles, or other sorts of cost sharing will apply. Although some of these decisions are set by state or federal laws, or by what packages insurers are willing to sell, many

of these decisions are up to the insurance purchaser—that is, usually, the employer. As a result, this second stage is often where
employers have the most influence, and where they face the biggest
risk of employees believing they have not been fair in their decisions.

Administration of Case-Specific Coverage Issues

The third stage is when a decision needs to be made about whether
a particular treatment will be covered for a particular person. For
example, this kind of case-specific decision occurs when an employee applies for preapproval for a nonemergency surgery or asks
for reimbursement for a new prescription drug or some other
treatment. In many cases, these decisions are dictated by the benefits design decisions that were already made. For example, if the
health care coverage clearly does not cover any cosmetic surgery,
case-specific decisions about rhinoplasty ("nose jobs") don't need
to be made, in most cases anyway (see the case titled "CodeRight's
Coverage Limits" in chapter 8 for an example of how designed
limits sometimes aren't as clearly defined as they might seem to
be).

Case-specific administration decisions often arise when there
is a dispute about whether something should be covered or not.
This can take place, for example, in the form of an appeal for
coverage. Sometimes these appeals revolve around esoteric insurance issues or somewhat opaque terms, like "medical necessity."
And for the most part, adjudicating case-specific appeals for coverage will be handled by the health plan, not the employer. But you
should still be concerned about appeals and how they are handled
for three reasons.

First, appeals decisions will often hinge on the design of the
package, over which you have a great deal of influence. If you
aren't satisfied with how appeals are turning out for you or your
employees, there might be something you can do about it by
changing the benefits design.

Second, employees who are not happy with how appeals are handled often complain to their employer. If enough of these complaints build up, employers have told us that they start thinking about changing insurance plans. After all, handling employee complaints is time-consuming, often emotionally challenging, and potentially expensive. On the other hand, changing plans can also be quite expensive, not to mention time-consuming, confusing, and disruptive for everyone concerned. So making sure that your company's health benefits are administered fairly, and that the appeals process works well, can save time and money in several ways.

Finally, some employers, especially large employers, are self-insured (they function as their own insurance plan). As a result, they may be more or less directly involved in administrative decisions, and even in adjudicating appeals. While small employers often work with a broker and usually are not involved in case-specific administrative decisions, we have heard of many cases where even small employers do become involved. They too might face the option of changing coverage on the spot (such as by expanding coverage for an individual who has reached a coverage limit), and therefore they, too, might end up having some degree of direct involvement in appeals.

Where to Apply the Five Ethical Guideposts

As we discuss the Five Ethical Guideposts for making fair health care coverage decisions, we will mostly keep these last two stages in mind. In many cases, both general benefits design decisions and case-specific administration decisions (see exhibit 1-2) should consider the same Five Ethical Guideposts. But for some Ethical Guideposts and in some cases, this will not be so. For example, broad employee participation (which we'll discuss in chapter 5) is very important for general benefits design, but it should not be a factor in most case-specific administration decisions. On the other hand, consistency (chapter 6) is an important Ethical Guidepost

EXHIBIT 1-2
TWO STAGES OF BENEFITS
DECISIONS

General Benefits Design Decisions

Benefits design decisions usually answer questions like, "What kind of coverage will be offered?" and "What treatments and prescriptions are covered?" When you decide to offer a specific preferred provider organization or health maintenance organization or health savings account, or when you decide that experimental treatments, or physical therapy, or long-term care will be covered, you are making benefits design decisions.

Case-Specific Administration Decisions

Case-specific decisions usually answer very specific questions that are not clearly addressed in the benefit design. For example, "Will our health plan cover travel to get a specific experimental chemotherapy for my child with leukemia?" Another real-life example is that, recently, physical rehabilitation has been used for children with epilepsy. This particular use of physical therapy is often not specifically mentioned in health insurance policies. The first time an employee brings a new treatment like this to you, you might have to make a case-specific coverage decision.

for both benefits design decisions and case-specific administration decisions.

In sum, how involved you are in general benefits design and case-specific decisions will depend on the way health care coverage is structured at your company. Companies that self-insure and only use insurance companies for administrative purposes might be involved every step of the way. This, however, is a bit unusual for smaller and midsize companies. More likely, you'll be most involved with benefits design and less involved with case-specific decisions. No matter how involved you are in case-by-case decisions, though, there are good reasons for you to make sure that all stages of health care coverage decisions are fair.

Legal Ramifications

If you need help determining your legal responsibilities and liabilities regarding the health care benefits you provide for your employees, you will need to find another book (and probably a lawyer!) to supplement this one. Legal requirements vary from state to state, and each business will have specific needs that we can't foresee or address. So, for example, *we can't and won't guarantee that following our advice will immunize you against lawsuits of any kind.* Of course, we hope that our recommendations will help you avoid trouble, including lawsuits, by maintaining good relationships with employees. But our primary purpose is to help you make fair decisions about health care coverage and therefore avoid disgruntled employees. If doing so also helps you to fulfill your legal obligations and avoid legal liability, well, that would be a welcome bonus.

The Ethical Guideposts Reflect Overlapping Ethical Principles

The Five Ethical Guideposts for making fair health care coverage decisions could be redefined in a number of ways, and it's pretty easy to imagine them as a somewhat longer or shorter list. For this book, we follow the lead of the Ethical Force Program (see exhibit 1-3) and their consensus report, *Ensuring Fairness in Health Care Coverage Decisions,* and separate out Five Ethical Guideposts:

EXHIBIT 1-3
THE ETHICAL FORCE PROGRAM™

The Ethical Force Program™ is a collaborative program that was created in 1997 by the Institute for Ethics at the American Medical Association. The program is overseen by a diverse group of leaders representing the perspectives of all the major participants in the health care system, from patients and physicians to health plans, regulators, and purchasers (see appendix A for a list). The Ethical Force Program has three general goals. First, it aims to identify shared standards for ethical behavior throughout the health care system. Second, it strives to develop valid, reliable, and feasible performance measures based on these shared ethical expectations. And third, it attempts to encourage the voluntary adoption of these standards and measures so that all parties in health care can be better held accountable to one another.

Health care coverage decisions should be transparent, participatory, consistent, sensitive to value, and compassionate.

As you'll immediately notice, these principles overlap and complement one another. They interlock or, more accurately, they flow together in the decision-making process. Unlike the pieces of a puzzle, the Five Ethical Guideposts for making fair health coverage decisions don't always have sharp lines of division. They are sometimes more akin to taking a warm fruit pie and slicing it into five pieces—you could make the cuts in different places, at different angles, for bigger or smaller slices. And though you can easily slide a knife between the pieces, as soon as the knife is gone, the contents of the slices want to flow together again.

One of the secrets to fair decision-making will be to take advantage of the way these principles overlap and flow together, and combine the strategies for, say, transparent and participatory decision-making, so that you work on both at the same time. As we move through the cases, we'll point out some general guidance to facilitate this kind of thinking, and we'll return to this point again at the end of the book.

Next Steps

Before we get to our detailed exploration of the Five Ethical Guideposts, in the next chapter we'll describe some of the most important reasons why it is wise for businesses to try to make the most fair health care coverage decisions possible. Of course, business ethics is a consideration, but there are also strong practical reasons to work on ensuring fairness in this particular decision-making process. Also, because the current health care system is often said to be unfair in general, we'll give a brief explanation of the current system and its historical origins.

▲

Why Worry?

The Business Case for Fair Decisions

*H*eather Rossi has been a successful restaurant owner in New Jersey for the last twenty-five years. Ten years ago she opened a second restaurant, and five years ago, a third. Now in the process of opening her fourth and fifth restaurants, she has decided to start offering health benefits—she hopes this will help her continue attracting the best employees. Over a couple of months, she spends much of her spare time digging through what feels like mountains of information and options, learning as much as she can about health benefits. Soon, however, she realizes that she is in over her head, and she brings in a consultant. By this point, the hiring process for the new restaurants has already started and is taking much of her time. So, guided by the consultant's expertise and based on her knowledge of her employees, Heather selects a plan. It doesn't have exactly the coverage she'd hoped for, nor the price she'd been aiming for, but she thinks this plan will be good enough to help her attract and retain good employees.

As the hiring process moves forward and she offers her new and existing employees this new benefit, she gives them a thick packet of information provided by the insurance company. Her very busy schedule keeps her from explaining the details of the *plan to each employee herself, but she has a quick meeting at each restaurant to explain the basic features of the plan and encourage employees to take advantage of this great new benefit. She closes each meeting by reminding everyone to read through the packets.*

It has now been six months since she started offering the health plan, and Heather is buried in paperwork. It seems that every other day an employee has a new complaint about the health plan. Some have cancelled their benefits. One has even raised the possibility of a lawsuit. The complaints include accusations of inconsistent coverage, incomprehensible rules, poor customer service, and out-of-pocket costs that are too high.

In response to these complaints, Heather starts surveying some of her employees about how to make the plan better. She learns a lot. For example, she finds out that many of her kitchen workers, from cooks to dishwashers, have opted against taking part in the health benefits. When pressed, many express confusion at the complexities of the packet and difficulties with reading it in English.

With a growing number of disgruntled employees, Heather starts to wish she had never offered the plan to begin with. She is now worried about losing employees and needs to find a new plan. But she's worried that she'll simply make the same mistakes again, or even make matters worse.

Heather finds herself in the middle of a tragic situation—she did the right thing by offering her employees health benefits. But because of the way she made her decisions, she now faces more unhappy employees than before. Sadly, we have learned through talking with hundreds of business owners and human resources professionals, this is not a rare scenario—especially for the owners of small but growing businesses.

Every year businesses large and small, old and new, examine the costs and value of providing or changing health benefits. Every year some businesses decide to offer benefits for the first time, or to change their existing benefits. And every year, some of these businesses make bad decisions about health benefits for their employees, and for their businesses.

In our view, there are two ways to evaluate any process for picking health care benefits. First, decisions about health coverage should be ethical, or to use a more straightforward term, they should be fair. We'll define "fairness" in more detail in later chapters, but for now think of fairness as being shorthand for all the parts of a decision that might make it more or less ethically sound (see exhibit 2-1). So, for example, a decision that is inequitable, that does not respect the integrity of the persons it affects and so on, would be unethical, or unfair.

Most employers believe strongly that they should offer only health plans that reflect very good ethics. In the words of one midsize employer, "If I ever thought that I was dealing with a plan that wasn't ethical, I don't care what it would offer, I would be somewhere else" (see appendix B). That strong belief that health care must be conducted ethically is why we're going to spend the rest of the book discussing how to ensure that the benefits you pick are ethical and fair.

Second, no business can succeed unless its decisions make good business sense. As much as businesses should make fair decisions because it's the right thing to do, we have also learned that the bottom line can be improved by making fair decisions about health care coverage. Over the last few years, we have conducted focus groups and interviews with business owners and leaders, human resources professionals, benefits consultants, and insurance brokers across the country. One thing has become increasingly clear: Making fair decisions about health care coverage has effects that reach far beyond the health care of any individual employee. It really can be healthy for the business too.

Currently, there are over 1,000 health insurance companies in the United States providing insurance for around 200 million workers. The federal government alone offers its employees around 300 different plans, adding new plans each year. More typically, though, employers must choose from among these many

EXHIBIT 2-1
WHAT'S FAIR?

Because we will be discussing it at great length throughout this book, it is appropriate to say a few things about fairness. As a concept in philosophy, fairness is most closely related to the notion of justice, or equity, and this is the primary sense in which we use the term in this book. For example, Aristotle initially described fairness as "treat equals equally and unequals unequally." This is essentially the kind of fairness this book will lead your health coverage decisions toward.

There are two important ethical implications of this sort of fairness, though. First, fairness for a group can sometimes seem unfair to an individual. For instance, in health care coverage decisions, being fair to a group of individuals sometimes requires denying an individual's request for benefits. Depending on what the benefit is, and as long as the same request would be denied to any individual of that group, this kind of denial might be fair. Second, in the case of health benefits, "equality," as Aristotle put it, actually has two important components. The first is equality in the kind of disease or symptom; the second is equality in the kind of coverage the employee selected. If two individuals have 20/100 vision, they might both have equal need for eyeglasses, but if one of them did not elect vision coverage, they don't have equal insurance plans. It might be fair for their coverage to be different because they are unequal, in terms of the plans they selected.

Despite their philosophical fairness, both of these situations can seem unfair to the people involved. After all, perhaps the employees who did not elect vision coverage could not afford it. If so, it's likely they also cannot afford the out-of-pocket costs of eyeglasses. And if one person is willing and able to go through an appeal to get coverage, while another isn't, then an appeals process that seems fair at the start might not be fair in how it actually works out. We'll see many more of these dilemmas as we progress through the book.

plans and then offer their employees just one or perhaps a few plans as options (see exhibit 2-2). Needless to say, this puts a lot of pressure on the employer, who is making decisions that can profoundly affect many employees and their families. If the employer ends up offering only a single option, the pressure is even greater to make sure the choice is a good one. But even if the employer makes lots of options available, that doesn't mean the pressure is off.

In general, after employers have spent time deciding which plan(s) to offer, employees are then given a month or so to pick among new and existing plans for the next year. Depending on a wide range of factors, each employee might be more or less successful in getting a good health plan for his or her own needs.

All these layers of complexity can give rise to both subtle and overt unfairness in the health care system. First of all, as we all know, many Americans go without health insurance coverage of any kind. Others receive coverage that is inadequate to meet their medical needs, leading to bankruptcies and innumerable medical tragedies. These situations are clearly unfair, and they reflect some underlying unethical aspects of our health care system. As someone who makes decisions about health care coverage, whether for a small, medium, or large business, it's important for you to do what you can to minimize the possibility of such unfairness for your own employees.

On your own, of course, you can't eliminate all unfairness in the health care system. But there are certain guideposts you can

EXHIBIT 2-2
EMPLOYERS COVERING EMPLOYEES

In 2005, 80 percent of all employers that offered benefits offered their employees a single plan, 14 percent offered two plans, and 6 percent offered three or more. This information can be misleading, however. Of Jumbo Firms (5,000+ workers), fully 65 percent offered three or more plans and only 17 percent offered a single plan. Conversely, only 5 percent of Small Firms (3–199 workers) offered three or more plans, while 81 percent offered only a single plan. Some other interesting information about benefits in 2005:

Small Firms (3–199): 59 percent offered benefits (of those, 81 percent offered a single plan, 14 percent two plans, and 5 percent three or more plans).

Medium Firms (200–1,000): 98 percent offered benefits (of those, 48 percent offered a single plan, 27 percent two plans, and 25 percent three or more plans).

Large Firms (1,000–5,000): virtually all offered benefits (of those, 27 percent offered a single plan, 24 percent two plans, and 49 percent three plans).

Jumbo Firms (5,000+): virtually all offered benefits (of those, 17 percent offered a single plan, 18 percent two plans, and 65 percent three or more plans).

All Firms: 60 percent offered benefits (of those, 80 percent offered a single plan, 14 percent two plans, and 6 percent three or more).

Workers (independent of type of firm): 37 percent could choose one plan, 20 percent could choose between two plans, and 43 percent could choose from three or more.

Source: Employer Health Benefits 2005 Annual Survey available at http://www.kff.org/insurance/7315/index.cfm (accessed March 13, 2006).

follow to help reduce the risks of unfairness—or perceived unfairness, which can be just as damaging—in your own decisions.

In sum, there are a lot of reasons why making decisions about health care coverage can be very difficult for both employers and employees. It's easy for either or both to make bad choices. In this book, we'll provide a number of examples where things went wrong, but we have also heard of times where things went well. Because even in the midst of a health care system that is at times unfair, it is possible for you, as the designer of health benefits for your employees, to make fair decisions.

The Five Ethical Guideposts
for Making Fair Decisions

Fair health coverage decisions will be transparent, participatory, consistent, sensitive to value, and compassionate. Making fair health coverage decisions can be aided by following these Five Ethical Guideposts. In the chapters that follow we will talk about each of these Ethical Guideposts in more depth. Here we provide a very brief explanation of each Ethical Guidepost and then explain how following them can be good for business.

Let's follow Heather as she considers possible new plans to offer. She can follow these Five Ethical Guideposts to improve health care coverage decisions for her, for her employees, and for her business.

Transparent

Decisions are transparent when the people who are affected by them, such as covered employees, know what the decisions are and know the reasons for them. *Transparency* is the first Ethical Guidepost because without transparency, your employees won't be able to understand the features of their health coverage and can't make good decisions. But it's also first because all the other Ethical Guideposts—*Participatory, Consistent, Sensitive to Value,* and *Compassionate*—require *Transparency* too. One way to ensure transparency in coverage decisions is to provide a number of informational forums for employees before and during enrollment periods. Heather should make sure that someone, even if it's not her, takes the time to explain the health coverage and the basis for it to her employees and answer their questions. Also, she should make reasonable accommodations for her employees who speak English as their second language. She may not be able to afford the cost of translating the information packet herself, but perhaps this is already available from the insurance company or health plan. Otherwise, intermediate steps to help them understand the benefits package should be made available. Offering a health benefit package won't help her recruit and retain good employees if they don't understand it.

Participatory

Employee participation in coverage decisions improves both the fairness and the legitimacy of coverage decisions, and it is especially important if tough choices need to be made (see exhibit 2-3). One of the goals of good health coverage is employee satisfaction, and employee participation in the decision process will help produce employee satisfaction. Finding out what employees value can help Heather to tailor coverage options so that they more accurately reflect what employees want. As we will discuss below, this doesn't mean offering coverage for services and care that are simply unavailable or not feasible given the resources available. But participation in the process can help employees to understand why

EXHIBIT 2-3
THE COSTS OF HEALTH
CARE DISPARITIES

There is a growing body of work on disparities in health care, particularly disparities between racial and ethnic groups. Recently, the National Business Group on Health produced an analysis for the Office of Minority Health in the U.S. Department of Health and Human Services that details the evidence, the costs, and the strategies to overcome these disparities in health care. One key thing this report recommends is that employers ask their employees about their experiences with the plan(s) and then use their responses as a guide for health plan renewals and changes.

Source: "Why Companies Are Making Health Disparities Their Business: The Business Case and Practical Strategies," *National Business Group on Health*, 2003; 14.

tough choices sometimes must be made. Heather was reluctant, at first, to involve her employees in the decision about which health plan to offer. But now she is having second thoughts. When her employees didn't know how much time and effort she spent on picking the plan, and why she made the choices she did, they got angry because the plan didn't live up to their expectations. This year, she is encouraging her employees to participate in the decision about changing the plan, by using an informal, anonymous survey of employee satisfaction with the current plan. She started by using the complaints she had already received, then she made a survey to find out if those complaints were widely shared, and what her employees would be willing to trade to get better health benefits. She is using the survey results in her talks at employee meetings to explain why the plan will be changing.

Consistent

Decisions must be consistent to meet the classic definition of fairness. Similar cases should be treated similarly, and different cases should be treated differently. Consistent decisions eliminate even an appearance of favoritism or punitive decision-making. And inconsistent decisions can lead to nasty legal troubles, such as discrimination lawsuits. As much as employees might want all their health problems covered, they also want to make sure someone else who has the same benefits is getting the same coverage. Heather has been hearing complaints of inconsistent coverage, but it's not clear from what has been said if Heather's coverage is really inconsistent or not. Her employees' complaints should certainly lead her to investigate this issue with the plan. If she finds the coverage has been inconsistent, that is something that should be fixed for the next year, or she will keep getting these complaints, one of which could turn into a lawsuit.

Sensitive to Value

When health care coverage decisions are sensitive to value, it improves the efficiency of the benefits offered. Most people want to get health care that is both effective (that works) and efficient (that works at a reasonable cost). Emphasizing coverage for those products and services that have clearly superior effectiveness and that get the most "bang for the buck" helps you and your employees spend money as efficiently as possible. How will Heather know if she is getting good value for her, and her employees', money? One place to look is at accreditation and performance information. Information from groups like the National Committee for Quality Assurance (NCQA) and their Health Plan Employer Data Information Set (HEDIS®) or the HealthGrades.com Web site might be particularly helpful as she evaluates different health plans. New sources of information are constantly being created to help employers sort out better value services and providers. Of course, today not all of this information is equally reliable or useful. But one thing is clear: Performance measures are becoming much more common in health care. Heather is going to want to find some trustworthy sources of information on the value offered by different plans and providers.

Compassionate

Health care coverage decisions need to have some degree of flexibility to offer individuals with unique health problems, with different health values, and with individual health goals the means to address their problems, to live in accordance with their values, and to achieve their goals. For good reason, employers and insurance companies want to avoid making exceptions from plan coverage rules. Thinking ahead about the likely needs of certain employee groups and incorporating flexibility into the coverage rules from the start are two ways to avoid the temptations of ad hoc exceptions later on. For example, whatever plan she chooses, Heather should make sure there is an adequate appeals process that is easy to understand, including for her non–English-speaking employees. She might also consider offering a plan option where she knows some of the providers can deliver care directly in other languages.

The Business Case

Why should Heather follow these Five Ethical Guideposts? The short answer is: for the same reasons she is now changing health plans. In fact, had she followed the Ethical Guideposts from the start, she might not need to go through the trouble and expense of changing plans now.

In general, businesses change health plans for one of three reasons. First, if the costs of an existing plan are no longer sustainable, employers can be forced to seek out a different, less expensive plan, even if they and their employees are satisfied with the services offered by the current plan. Second, if a plan no longer exists as it once did—if the plan goes out of business, or even just changes the rules of eligibility or coverage, or the hospitals and physicians that it works with—many employers will need to change plans to try to maintain something similar to what the old plan offered. Third, growing employee dissatisfaction can drive employers to change plans. In some ways, this last reason might be the most frustrating, because it is also the most avoidable. Costs will go up, and plans can change with little warning, but if employees are gradually becoming more and more dissatisfied, a good employer should not be caught by surprise. And an excellent employer will be able to head off problems like this before they get out of hand.

In an ideal situation, businesses pick or design health benefits they will not have to change. At worst, they hope to make small annual changes in response to changing employee preferences, market options, and so on. This just makes good business sense. Changing plans every year takes time, money, and energy, and can be an inefficient use of any business's resources.

How employees think about, respond to, and feel about their health plan is due in part to the kind of plan it is, but it is also related to how the plan was chosen and then presented to them. In other words, an important way to limit the number of times you have to change plans is to work toward employee understanding and satisfaction about how the plan was chosen. Employee understanding of the process and the decision leads to appropriate expectations, and appropriate expectations lead to satisfaction. Or, to put it another way, inappropriate expectations will almost always lead to dissatisfaction.

Like Heather, you can use the Five Ethical Guideposts to help your employees understand how health benefits are chosen and to set reasonable expectations. The Ethical Guideposts should also lead to more fair coverage decisions, which will lead to higher degrees of employee satisfaction.

Of course we can't guarantee complete employee satisfaction, but we learned from our interviews and focus groups that employees are more likely to be satisfied with their health plans if the Ethical Guideposts are followed.

Employee satisfaction with their health benefits is important for reasons that go beyond the potential waste of resources in changing health benefits more frequently. Sure, it can save money if employees are satisfied and you don't have to change plans every year, but employee satisfaction with the health plan is important for other business reasons as well.

• The number of appeals and complaints will be affected by employee satisfaction. We've heard over and over that every employer encounters an occasional employee who complains about every pea under the mattress. Of course this employee is probably going to have a complaint and file an appeal regardless of the benefits you choose to offer. We're not aiming to avoid that appeal. Instead, we want you to avoid the potential landslide of appeals and complaints about policies that appear to be (or are) unfair, unrealistic, or incomprehensible. Think back to Heather Rossi. If her initial attempt to choose a health plan had followed the Five Ethical Guideposts, she (and her employees) might have spent less time dealing with problems, limitations, and complaints about the plan.

• Retention rates are affected by employee satisfaction with the health plan. Research has shown that tying health coverage to employment has limited employee turnover,[1] but every once in a while in conversation you hear two people comparing health benefits: "Well, my friend Shaun didn't have to pay for his tetanus shot, but I had to pay almost $200." Considering all you might have read over the years about health insurance "job-lock," it might seem counterintuitive to think that individuals would change jobs in order to get better health benefits. But as health care costs continue to rise, and more direct costs are carried by employees, more and more individuals are likely to do so. Imagine a worker who is about to start a family. If your benefits package will not meet his or her growing family's needs, he or she will start looking for a job that will. In Heather's case, she knows that not many restaurants offer health benefits. So she is trying to take advantage of the fact that some good employees will come to work for her because of this new benefit. At the same time, she now knows how important it is to do it right, or this wonderful new benefit could get the best of her.

• Employee productivity is also affected by their satisfaction with their benefits. Research shows that employees who feel they are being treated unjustly tend to put in less effort, because they lose their sense of loyalty and trust with the business.[2] Other research shows that the number of sick days an employee takes is affected by how fairly she believes she is being treated at work. And it is not just *feeling* like one is being treated unfairly that leads to skipping out from work—it is real illness. In other words, employees who believe they are being treated unfairly don't just take more days off work, they actually get sick more often.[3]

Two-Step Decisions

Despite all the potential issues we've outlined, for many employers picking a health plan is often not as complicated as it might seem. As we discussed in chapter 1, picking a health plan has two phases: general benefits design and case-specific benefits administration. Although they are very different stages of the health coverage decision process, both can significantly affect the degree to which your employees see the process as being fair.

First, setting the premiums, deductibles, covered benefits, and percentage of services paid by the employee and by the plan is the benefits design stage. This stage ends before employees are given actual concrete choices about plans to choose. Businesses are likely to be most closely involved in this phase of the process. Larger businesses, which tend to be self-insured, will have the most decisions to make. But even smaller businesses will usually have many plans to choose from, with varying levels of premiums, co-payments, deductibles, and so on. All of the Ethical Guideposts apply to this stage of the health coverage process.

Second, determining whether or not a filed claim will be covered, or adjudicating appeals for coverage, occurs at the administrative step. Some businesses that self-insure will have a direct role in some of these decisions. Most businesses that contract with an insurer will be much less involved, if at all. But every business can become involved in appeals if an employee calls on you for help. Many of the business leaders we've spoken to relate stories of employees who needed their help in dealing with a health insurance issue. Having a process for handling these sorts of requests that is transparent, participatory, consistent, sensitive to value, and perhaps especially, compassionate can avert some of the most serious potential problems an employer can face regarding health insurance.

Abuse or Misuse of the Ethical Guideposts

The Five Ethical Guideposts are meant to provide help in choosing the best health plans for you and your employees. We have been asked about something, though: What if the Ethical Guideposts, as well-intended as they are, were to be misused?

In many cities throughout the country, pedestrian signals on stoplights include a numeric countdown from the "walk" to the "don't walk" signal. This information is clearly intended to help pedestrians know how long they have to get across the intersection. But it can also be used by motorists to speed through a light as it is about to turn red, or to get a head start on a light before it turns green. That is, they can use this information in ways that it wasn't intended to be used.

In the same way, it seems possible that a business could try to use the Ethical Guideposts we have provided merely as public relations cover. In a worst-case scenario, the decision-making process could be opaque, unilateral, discriminatory, inattentive to value, and inflexible, but the employer decides to fake attention to the Five Ethical Guideposts in an effort to fool the employees into believing the process is transparent, participatory, consistent, sensitive to value, and compassionate.

Now obviously, we do not intend to provide advice on creating a cover for unfair decision-making. But more importantly, we don't think it would work. It might be possible, but we think it would be very hard to completely fake paying attention to the Ethical Guideposts.

Here's why. Once the process of *pretending* to seek the most fair decisions possible about health coverage has started, it is likely to take on a life of its own. That is to say, just going through the motions of paying attention to these Ethical Guideposts might be enough, in the end, to produce the right kinds of decisions.

Imagine a benefits decision-maker who decides that she just wants her decision process to look like it is participatory (see chapter 5), but she has already decided what to do—so there is no *real* opportunity for employee input. In order to make it appear participatory, she will have to make it possible for employees to provide input (which, granted, she intends to ignore), make the necessary announcements (otherwise, employees won't even know she is trying to fool them into believing she is operating a participatory process), and actually collect input from her employees. Having done all this, she will then have some information at hand that could actually make the process participatory. Why not use it? What's more, because she has set up a structure and process for soliciting input, her employees are likely to expect that the benefits decisions will reflect this input or at least that reasons will be provided as to why they don't. So you see, merely by going through the motions of the process, she is now in a position to be held accountable for taking seriously employee participation.

Most importantly, though, once this imaginary decision-maker has this information, it will be clear that it makes better business sense to use it. After all, why not craft the fairest possible health benefits package? Ignoring the input will cost her whatever she spent on collecting it, will put at risk any trust she gained in doing so, and is liable to have negative effects on her retention rates and employee productivity.

"Give Him an Inch and He'll Take a Mile": The Importance of Balancing the Ethical Guideposts

Another objection we've heard is that if employees are involved in these decisions, they'll ask for everything, expectations will be raised that can never be fulfilled, and dissatisfaction will result when they feel their input has been ignored.

This arises from a misunderstanding of how to use the Ethical Guideposts and what they mean. Several times in this chapter and elsewhere we have discussed employee satisfaction. We've also discussed what employees want in their health care benefits— including attention to their health values and priorities. At times it may even seem that we describe these as the same—employees can only be satisfied with the decision-making process when they are given what they want. But from our interviews, we know that this just isn't true. What is important is that employees understand how decisions are made, and that those decisions are made in a rational way, using criteria that almost all employees would agree on. A process like this will have credibility. It will have legitimacy. And even if it then turns out (as it almost certainly will) that the resulting health plan doesn't meet every individual's specific wants, it is likely to be accepted because it was based on a legitimate, credible process.

For example, think about the differences between traditional medicine and alternative medicine. Day-to-day health coverage decisions are usually confined to traditional medical practices, but let's say that a growing number of your employees would like your health insurance to cover alternative therapies. Specifically, let's assume they are asking for coverage for homeopathy. At first glance at the Ethical Guideposts, it might seem like refusing to cover homeopathic treatments in the face of employee requests to do so would be unfair and would produce unsatisfied employees (see chapter 5, on the Ethical Guidepost, *Participatory*).

But then you should look further into the guideposts. None of them works in a vacuum; they need to be balanced against each other. Here, for instance, you would also need to consider the Ethical Guidepost, *Sensitive to Value* (chapter 7). Now, in some cases, research has shown that alternative therapies actually are valuable. Chiropractors in combination with traditional medical practice are sometimes more successful at treating back pain than traditional medicine alone, for example. For the most part, though, alternative therapies like homeopathy have unknown effectiveness. Given this, there is a credible, legitimate rationale for not covering homeopathic treatments.

While this case is entirely hypothetical, we've heard many examples of similar cases. In many of them, reasonable compromises are reached, generally on the basis of recognizing the importance of balancing complementary Ethical Guideposts.

Will the Guideposts Really Work?

For both employers and employees, the most difficult challenge to making fair health care coverage decisions is that doing so sometimes costs money and time. These resources must be added to the resources already expended on the health coverage itself. This can be particularly frustrating for some employers, especially those who believe that health care benefits should not be their responsibility—and there are many in this camp. In the next chapter, we will briefly review the curious history of health care coverage in the United States. For now, suffice it to say that some employers today take responsibility for health care coverage for their employees simply because the labor market demands it; others do so because they get many other benefits from it. Members of the Ethical Force Program and many others recognize that whenever an employer takes on responsibility for health care coverage—whether voluntarily, reluctantly, or with a sense of social purpose—it raises several important considerations.

These considerations have also arisen as possible objections to trying to use the Ethical Guideposts for decision-making.

Employers and Their Employees Are in an Unequal Power Relationship

Health care coverage decisions will always be molded in power relationships and, usually, the employees are at a disadvantage, at least in the short run. For example, no matter how much you might try to foster employee participation, this participation will be shaped by the fact that you hold the key to your employees' paychecks. And the reality is that not all employees will be willing to complain or even to make suggestions for improvement. This power imbalance is somewhat mitigated by the fact that business owners and human resources personnel are usually covered under the same plans as other employees—so their participation sometimes reflects the experiences of the other employees. After all, everyone involved has an incentive to find a fair coverage plan. But still, some employees who could provide valuable feedback might be reluctant to get involved for fear of making waves.

This is a serious concern, but it does not remove the possibility of meaningful contributions by employees. Instead, it means that employers should be especially attentive to the effect of the unequal power relationship on the way employees participate and the way that participation is handled. For example, it might help to provide anonymous opportunities for feedback or to have a third party collect the information. In short, recognizing the unequal power relationship makes attention to the Ethical Guideposts for fair decision-making all the more important.

Employer Decisions Will Always Be Driven, Ultimately, by Cost

No matter how much employers may want to make fair decisions, this argument suggests, the final judgment will always have to be reconciled to the bottom line.

In one regard, this makes perfect sense. It does neither the employer nor the employee any good to have fair decisions about health coverage from a business that goes out of business. So, cost is a very serious concern. But our interviews suggest that there is a good deal of variation in how costs come into play in making health care benefits choices. Sometimes cost is a primary driver, but as often as not, cost is just one consideration among many. After all, the people making these decisions often have to live with the same choices for their health coverage too. Factors like employee satisfaction, the risks of having to change plans again, avoiding emotionally devastating complaints, and the plain desire to do the right thing, all can come into play. It is not at all uncommon to hear from employers that they have adjusted the health coverage they offer to help meet specific employee needs, even sometimes for employees who are very sick and are unlikely to return to work. Such actions are clearly not purely cost-driven. They do, however, have long-term business benefits, because they build a sense of solidarity and loyalty among employees toward the business.

The Ethical Guideposts Are Too Ambiguous to Provide Any Real Guidance

This objection has been most common when business people first glance at the Five Ethical Guideposts. Take for example the final Ethical Guidepost, *Compassion* (chapter 8). When we ask employers whether they should be compassionate in the health care coverage they provide, who could say no? But it might be impossible to know whether these same employers actually are paying attention to this value when they put together their health benefits package—or so the argument goes.

It turns out, however, that there are some measurable steps a business can take that can signify compassion. Of course there aren't perfect measures of compassion—this isn't mathematics, it's business ethics we're talking about. But just because the measures of compassion are indirect and imperfect doesn't mean they are useless. For one thing, at minimum, if a business is *not* taking any of the measurable steps we will lay out, it might be fair to say that compassion is not a primary value in its decision-making process. And the same can be said for the steps we will lay out for the other Ethical Guideposts: *Transparency, Participatory, Consistent,* and *Sensitive to Value.*

Conclusion

There are a number of important reasons why businesses should care about having a fair process for choosing health care benefits. The reasons range from ethical concerns, like developing a strong sense of community within the business, to purely financial concerns, like the high costs associated with changing health plans if a bad choice is made. As Heather Rossi found out in our case example for this chapter, basing these critical decisions on guesswork about what employees want and need can lead to major problems for a business.

As we all know, there is no universally perfect health plan. In large part, this is because the perfect health plan to one person can seem like a flawed plan to someone else. Each of us might wish for a slightly different health plan, given our own needs, values, and priorities. As a result, the imperfections your employees find in any health plan may be surprising or they may be expected, but they will always find imperfections. Accordingly, the recommendations provided here cannot show businesses, no matter how big or small, how to get the perfect health plan for all employees. Instead, they show the process for making decisions that will provide most of your employees most of the time with good and fair health benefits.

Notes

1. S. Adams, "Employer-provided health insurance and job change," *Contemporary Economic Policy,* 22(3): 2004; 357–369.

2. *MetLife's Employee Benefits Trend Survey*, 2003.

3. M. Kivimaki, J. Ferrie, E. Brunner, J. Head, M. Shipley, J. Vahtera, M. Marmot, "Justice at work and reduced risk of coronary heart disease among employees," *Archives of Internal Medicine*, 165(19): 2005; 2245–2251.

▲

Why Is Health Insurance for Employees My Problem, Anyway?

A Brief History of Health Insurance Coverage in the United States

*J*ohn Barker is the human resources manager with primary responsibility for soliciting and choosing health care coverage options for employees at Stedman, Stedman, and Epstein, a law firm
with almost 1,000 employees. Over the years, he has used a number of different strategies to select plans, including working with
insurance brokers and sifting through information provided by
various independent health plan evaluation services. This year,
he's planning on making just a few tweaks to the existing set of
plans. The changes are mainly due to plan-initiated modifications
on what procedures and services will be covered under each plan,
but small increases in co-pays are also in the works. Right now the
law firm offers a health maintenance organization (HMO), three
preferred provider organizations (PPOs), and an indemnity plan.
John has carefully tailored the three PPOs to provide three differ-

ent levels of coverage at three different premium, co-payment, and deductible levels.

Of course John is also an employee of Stedman, Stedman, and Epstein. Each year he, like all other employees, must decide on the health plan he'll use for the coming year. He has been pretty happy for the past several years with PPO #2, which has a modest premium and also modest deductibles and co-payments. He has also established a consistent amount to put in his Health Care Flexible Spending Account (HCFSA) each year. For each of the last three years, he has put aside $500 to cover deductibles and other uncovered health care expenses—and every year this seems to be just enough. This year, however, things might be different because John and his wife, Michelle, are expecting another child two months before open enrollment is set to begin.

Fortunately, John and Michelle's son Trevor is born healthy. When open enrollment arrives, John tries to balance keeping an affordable premium while also putting aside a reasonable amount in his HCFSA. His main concern is predicting the likely health care costs that he and his family will accrue throughout the year. In the end, John decides to stick with his modest premium, modest deductible PPO, but he increases his HCFSA contribution to $1,000 per year. All things considered, this seems to John like a very reasonable package for a healthy, growing family.

Two months into the new year of coverage, however, Michelle seeks treatment for headaches. Their doctor thinks she is having migraine headaches, but traditional treatments for migraines aren't working very well. Tests don't show any other explanations for her headaches, and their family doctor is stumped, as are the allergist and neurologist she is referred to. They suggest that perhaps stress and sleeplessness, which are common following childbirth, are playing a role in her headaches. After several months, Michelle seeks help from a massage therapist and an acupuncturist. Finally, a blend of massage, acupuncture, and traditional therapies does the trick.

Despite multiple claim submissions and attempts to appeal,

John and Michelle are unable to procure reimbursement for her massage therapy or acupuncture fees from PPO#2. Looking back on his decision, John wishes he had opted for PPO#3, which has a higher premium but at least would have covered massage therapy. And the $1,000 in their HCFSA? It was spent after the first five months of the coverage year.

As the case of John and Michelle shows, selecting a health care package is complicated. First of all, most employees have to choose a health plan from among those someone else has picked as options. In fact, many employers give their employees only one plan to choose from—so John and Michelle are actually pretty lucky. They are also lucky because John is well aware of how health plans work. As the human resources director, he has spent a lot of time examining health plans. Most employees don't know nearly as much about how health care coverage works.

More importantly, though, a lot of employees—and maybe even John, too—tend to assume that all health plans cover basically the same things and are different only in their premiums, co-payments, and deductibles. If something unexpected comes up, they just figure (or hope) that whatever health care services they need will be covered.

This case shows that not all health plans cover the same services and treatments. And even an expert with lots of choices can end up picking the wrong plan.

Despite being very knowledgeable about choosing health plans, John still made a mistake. That's because choosing a health plan always involves some degree of speculation. No one can know exactly what health needs they will have in the coming year, nor will they know in advance the best way to meet those needs. As it turned out, John and Michelle would have been better off if they had elected a different coverage, such as PPO#3, or maybe even by choosing a plan with a lower premium but then making a higher contribution to their HCFSA.

At the same time, this case doesn't begin to touch on other

complexities of the health care system. It doesn't mention whether Stedman, Stedman, and Epstein is self-insured under the Employment Retirement Income Security Act (ERISA) (though they are, which puts John in the peculiar situation of being both the insurer and the insured in this case). It also doesn't give details about his plan's prescription coverage, the appeals process they went through, other aspects of coverage that might matter for John and his family (such as dental, vision, or disability insurance), and whether Michelle has other insurance options, perhaps from her own employer.

All of these factors could further complicate what benefits to choose as John tries to balance his own needs and those of all the other employees of Stedman, Stedman, and Epstein. And wrong decisions can cost a lot. An employee who makes a wrong decision can be stuck with thousands of dollars in bills. Health care costs are the leading cause of personal bankruptcies in the United States.

As John's case also shows, these decisions aren't just hard for employees; they are tricky and costly for employers too. As the person responsible for selecting plans to offer, John undoubtedly knows that for the employer each piece of a health care coverage package might require separate decisions about whether to acquire the coverage, whether to charge employees separately for it, whether to include alternative means of coverage, and so on. One wrong decision can lead to employee frustrations, which sometimes are taken out on him.

This chapter gives a brief overview of health insurance in America. But it is not a litany of every type of insurance or a guide on how to coordinate various insurance products for your employees. Given the rapidly changing face of health coverage (see, for example, the relatively recent introduction of Health Savings Accounts and the new Medicare part D drug coverage), a great deal of this kind of advice may be outdated by the time you get to the next chapter. Instead, we are going to focus on a short tour of the history of employer-sponsored health insurance coverage in the United States and then discuss the general goals of managed care health plans.

Though insurance plans can and do change dramatically over time, the general goals of employer-sponsored health plans have remained relatively constant for more than fifty years. Accordingly, the goal of this chapter is twofold: Identify the reasons employer-based health insurance coverage has been so resilient, and recognize the tension points within the managed care coverage system that will come into play in making decisions about health care coverage.

Health Insurance in the United States

Even one hundred years ago, some precursors to community-based health insurance, HMOs and other managed care organizations had popped up around the United States (see exhibit 3-1). Most of these were simply community fundraisers. For example, community members might be given the option to purchase shares of a new hospital project and, in return, they would receive discounted medical care at the hospital.

In the 1940s, the first direct ancestors of today's HMOs were created and became fairly successful. Kaiser Permanente in California, the Group Health Cooperative of Puget Sound in Seattle, Washington, and the Health Insurance Plan of New York all became solid market contenders. At the time, most health insurers offered what we would now call very traditional insurance, with open-ended coverage—usually covering about 80 percent of any medical bill submitted from any physician. What made these forerunners of the modern HMO unique, therefore, was their attempt to control costs and improve community health by restricting their members' access to only those physicians who were employed by (or under contract with) the group. These physicians, in turn, were expected to work together closely to provide cost-effective care to the whole group. Often, this meant working together on public health or preventive care programs, for example.

EXHIBIT 3-1
HEALTH INSURANCE IN THE
UNITED STATES—A TIMELINE

1900–1920: Health insurance is almost nonexistent.

1920–1940: Rising costs of medical care led to increasing demand and introduction of insurance. Introduction of pre-paid hospitalization and prepaid physician services—a type of insurance.

1935: Social Security Act passes, but without national health insurance, which had originally been part of the legislation.

1940–1960: Commercial insurance companies enter the market and increasing use of technological advances leads to continued higher costs.

1943: War Labor Board permits employers to offer health insurance as a fringe benefit to offset a wage freeze.

1949: Supreme Court allows collective bargaining for employment-based health insurance.

1965: Medicare and Medicaid are passed.

1974: Employment Retirement Income Security Act (ERISA) enacted, allowing employers to serve as their own insurers and exempting these "self-insured" health insurance plans from state insurance regulations.

1974: HMO Act supports growth of managed care.

1986: Consolidated Omnibus Budget Reconciliation Act (COBRA) guarantees that workers who leave their jobs can buy insurance through their former employer for 18 months.

1996: Health Insurance Portability and Accountability Act gives workers the right to buy COBRA coverage that covers preexisting conditions.

2003: Medicare drug bill creates tax-advantaged health savings accounts.

Although these pioneers of managed care were able to establish themselves as a small part of American medical care, for a variety of reasons (including opposition by the medical profession—see exhibit 3-2), they remained small in scale until the late 1980s.

EXHIBIT 3-2
WHY DID ORGANIZED MEDICINE
OPPOSE THE EARLY HMOs?

Since the creation of the AMA in 1847, doctors have been worried about becoming employees of companies rather than working directly for patients. The original concerns related to "company doctors" at the turn of the last century, who were widely seen as pawns of wealthy industrialists and who often did not serve the needs of their patients. This concern translated directly to the early HMOs, some of which were created by industrialists to provide care to their employees. Although doctors' mistrust of health plans has been reduced in more recent times, in other ways mistrust of HMOs has continued to grow—among both doctors and the general public. In short, ethical concerns about the influence on doctors of being the employee of a corporation remain high today.

One reason the early HMOs didn't grow very rapidly until the 1980s was the lack of real economic pressure to reduce health care costs before then. Through the middle parts of the twentieth century, health care was seen as a good place to spend money and health care costs weren't rising so fast that the general public would become concerned. Major technological improvements were happening, which bolstered public support for spending money on medical care, and these new technologies were spreading slowly enough that costs rose at acceptable levels. For example, the first iron lung was used successfully in 1927, the first successful use of the heart-lung machine was in 1953 (which made possible the first bypass surgery at that time), and the first pacemaker was used in 1961. All of these technologies were seen as providing miraculous cures, but none became widely used or available until decades after their first uses.

Many of the early efforts to provide discounted health care were also pressured out of existence by physician groups. In one famous case, the Supreme Court ruled that the American Medical Association violated antitrust laws when it tried to pressure a Washington, D.C., health care cooperative out of existence. Though these efforts by physicians to close early HMOs were generally portrayed, by doctors, as being driven by concerns about professional autonomy, critics saw it otherwise. They noticed that doctors employed by these groups were generally paid a salary, which didn't always match up to the fees that independent doctors were able to charge. Doctors responded with the concern that salaried physicians might be less motivated than those paid a fee for service. (See exhibit 3-2.) And so the arguments raged and early HMOs remained a very small part of the American health care system for many decades after they were first created.

This is not to say that health coverage in the United States was static from before World War II to the eventual rise of managed care in the 1980s and 1990s. The war itself was an important catalyst for a shift in health coverage that led to our current system. During the war, there was a tremendous labor shortage, as able-bodied men were inducted into military service. Employers became desperate for workers, and wages started to rise dramatically before the federal government mandated a wage freeze to try to keep the economy stable during wartime. Employers must have been grateful, but the wage freeze didn't solve their labor problems. They still needed, somehow, to lure scarce employees to work for them. Fierce competition for employees led employers to search for new ways to lure workers away from the competition. Health care insurance became one such lure.

Very soon, most major employers had begun to incorporate health insurance coverage as part of their nonwage "benefits package" for employees. This decision was solidified later in the 1940s when the IRS decided that health insurance contributions made by employers on behalf of an employee would not be counted as wages for the employee's income taxes. Meanwhile, the employer could write off the full cost of the insurance as a business expense. The net effect of this decision was that employer contributions to health benefits were of greater economic value to employees than were increases in salary of the same dollar amount. For instance, at a 25 percent income tax rate, an employer could, for the same cost, either offer an employee a $75 raise in take-home pay or give them a $100 increase in health benefits. Labor unions were aware of this, and they negotiated better and better health insurance packages for their members.

You might be surprised to hear that the establishment of Medicare and Medicaid in 1965 initially did very little to change the *nature* of health insurance coverage. These programs brought huge numbers of new people into the health care system with insurance, but they operated entirely according to the existing fee-for-service insurance system. As a result, they did not initially affect the types of insurance coverage available. Eventually, however, the introduction of Medicare and Medicaid was very influential, because the programs brought the issue of cost to the fore in a new way. Government was now in a position where it would need to address the tension between the cost of health care and the aim of covering as many people as possible. Since the beginning, Medicare and Medicaid have been in constant struggle to balance costs and coverage.

In the 1970s, health coverage began to take a very dramatic shift. At that time, technological innovation and fee-for-service health coverage was leading to rising numbers of medical specialists with expensive services to offer. Though these expensive services were often effective and very popular, rising costs began to be noticed by the public and politicians. It would be another decade before costs became issues of great national concern, but passage of the HMO Act in 1974 was motivated by cost worries, and it led to a bolstering of the HMOs' foothold in the market.

By the 1980s, health care costs were widely agreed to be out of control. The traditional fee-for-service scheme of simply covering every medical product or service according to physicians' judgments and so-called "usual and customary" fees was not sustainable without huge annual increases in insurance costs. In the latter half of the decade, an increase of 14 percent in the cost of health insurance was considered a good year for many employers. It eventually became common to note that U.S. automobile manufacturers spend more on health insurance per car than they do on steel. In times like these, HMOs and a growing variety of other types of managed care plans began to look much more appealing than they had in the middle of the century. The stage was set for the rapid growth of managed care, which promised to restrain costs while retaining or even improving health care quality.

With rapidly increasing costs and continuing employee expectations of excellent health coverage, the struggle to balance costs and coverage became every company's problem and a problem for every employee, even though most of them might not have known it. Insurance companies kept raising premiums, and employers ended up suppressing wages in order to be able to cover the rising costs of health insurance coverage. Though many employees didn't realize it, the basic economics of employer-sponsored health insurance had not changed since World War II: Health insurance was (and still is) a substitute for wages.

Tensions Within Managed Care

It would be misleading to say that managed care aims only to control costs, since quality control is also a common concern. But there is little doubt that the impetus for the rise of managed care came from the desire to rein in out-of-control health care costs. But how did costs get so out of control? Health care and health care insurance operate on the same market principles as other goods (including other types of insurance), don't they?

We mentioned technology, and the increasing number of physician specialists to deliver that technology, as one reason why costs have risen so dramatically in health care since the 1970s. The aging of the population is another reason, since older people generally use more health care services. But neither of these makes health care all that different from a number of other areas, where technology has changed things or where changes in the population can affect the demand for services. Unlike in health care, computer prices have actually come down as technologies have advanced, for example. And spending on health care is rising far faster than the aging of the population alone would predict.

Another important factor in rising health care costs is patient insulation from these costs. When an employer arranges for health insurance for their employees, the employees often believe that they are not paying (or not paying fully) for the health insurance they have or for health care services they receive. A general lack of awareness of the costs of health care (the opposite of cost-conscious purchasing, what could be called "cost-unconsciousness") results directly from this structure. Employees are literally unaware of the costs of health benefits and of their health care, which can lead to demand for services that they would not otherwise be willing to pay for themselves. And because many people (even doctors!) are often unaware of what each specific service costs, it is common for physicians and patients to make decisions about whether to order a test, or try a course of therapy with a new drug, while being blissfully unaware of the costs.

Another contributing factor toward increasing costs was that doctors did not take it upon themselves to restrain spending. Of course, there was little reason for them to do so, at least as long as increased spending contributed something to their patients' health. And it doesn't hurt to be paid more for spending more, as was the case for much of the twentieth century in American medicine. The tradition of professional autonomy of medical practitioners also played a role. Doctors simply did not see it as part of their role to restrain medical spending; they saw their role as being independent protectors of the health of their patients. And many doctors still see it this way. Today, most physicians (quite reasonably, in our view) expect that their *primary* responsibility is to provide optimal care to their patients, not to save money for a health insurance plan or an employer. And it is probably fair to say that most patients like it that way. On the other hand, there are obvious consequences when doctors are put in charge of spending, but they believe that their *only* duty is to provide the best possible care, no matter the cost.

How much responsibility for controlling costs should fall to doctors? This quintessential dilemma of modern medical ethics has yet to be fully resolved—and it is the subject of a number of other books. Fortunately, we won't have to resolve this issue here, since our focus is on the role of purchasers. But that doesn't mean the role of doctors and other practitioners in making sure coverage decisions are fair isn't important.

A final important contributing factor, which we're somewhat more interested in for the purposes of this book, is the misuse of medical resources, which often occurs out of ignorance. When medical care is misused out of malice or greed, of course, that is a crime (such as fraud), and though fraud undoubtedly contributes something to high medical costs, it is not a primary concern for us here. But medical resources can also be misused because it is not clear what the most effective type of test or treatment is for a certain patient or group of patients. This problem will be discussed more in chapter 7. For now, we note that physician autonomy in the care of patients has remained an important feature of medical care, but before the rise of evidence-based medicine (EBM—a movement to ground medical practice in scientific studies), researchers discovered that the use of medical services was extremely unpredictable. A patient with the same illness might receive dramatically different treatments in different regions of the country, and sometimes even between one hospital and the hospital next door.

Without the benefit of good research on medical treatments, and ways to get the word out about what works and what doesn't, the "standard of care" for doctors could, and did, vary widely. Without a broadly agreed-upon standard of care, physicians end up treating some patients unnecessarily, treating similar patients differently, and generally misallocating health care resources. These problems have not been solved to anyone's satisfaction, though things are certainly getting better. Work in this area is important to ensure that the medical services covered are the ones most likely to help improve your employees' health.

Managed care, at its apex, seemed poised to address all of these factors. More recently, though, it seems that newer solutions—which might be thought of as either an evolution in managed care or perhaps a revolution away from managed care, depending on your point of view—are also being sought, because some of these issues have been intractable.

Over the last twenty years, managed care plans have used a number of strategies to raise awareness of costs and encourage efficiency in the use of health care services. As a result, while managed care has become a fixture of health coverage, many employees have become more aware of the costs of medical care. Much of this was at the encouragement of employers, who were trying to keep costs down, but they were mainly carried out by health plans. Today, employers are getting more directly involved in these efforts. For example, one newer way to raise employee awareness of costs has been to set a clear limit on how much the employer will spend on health insurance coverage—this is sometimes called a "defined contribution" approach to offering health insurance. Following this strategy, employers allot a certain number of coverage dollars to each employee. Once these coverage dollars are expended, employees are responsible for covering any additional costs. Whether this counts as a managed care strategy or not doesn't really matter. It is an example of employers starting to see cost control as something they need to be proactive about.

Other new developments have occurred in the ways that doctors and other health professionals, as well as the organizations where they work, are encouraged to be more efficient in their use of resources. For example, an older means of encouraging efficiency among health care providers was to cap how much to pay for particular procedures. Hospitals would be able to charge only a set amount for any patient admitted to the hospital with a certain diagnosis, regardless of how much it actually costs to take care of that patient (this is called using "Diagnosis-Related Groups," or DRG payments). Another older method is that doctors who sign up to participate in a health insurance plan are often paid a preset amount for each service they provide. This "fee-schedule" approach to cost control has been widely decried by doctors, especially as it has been used for Medicaid and Medicare insurance plans where the set fee sometimes doesn't cover the actual cost of care. Newer ideas are on the way, though. They include paying doctors or hospitals extra if they meet quality or cost benchmarks—the so-called "pay for performance" approach.

These new systems are complex and come with both potential benefits and risks. Almost certainly, some will work better than others. The point here is that concerns about providing high-quality care at a reasonable cost are not going away. As a result, the health care coverage system, both inside and outside of managed care plans, is continuing to evolve.

At this point, it may be most accurate to describe managed care itself as a modest success, one with good reasons for its failures. Patients, in general, still remain relatively insulated from the costs of medical care. On the one hand, this means they can continue to demand more than they or their employers can afford. On the other hand, insulating the ill from the immediate costs of their care is what health insurance is all about. It might be that balancing individual responsibility and the protection of the most vulnerable is a task that managed care alone could not accomplish.

The Ethical Role of Businesses in Providing Health Insurance Coverage

While academics and policy makers continue to debate the best ways to provide health coverage to U.S. citizens in the future, employers must make decisions today about how to provide health insurance coverage to their employees. Some claim that it would be much easier for employers if the United States were to adopt a single-payer, government-sponsored, system. Whether you are for or against this idea (and plenty of people don't want government to make decisions about health care), it is true that a government-run system would probably relieve employers from making tough decisions about health benefits and what to cover or not to cover. But it is also true that for now, and we suspect for some time to come, employer-sponsored health insurance coverage will remain a fact of business in America (see exhibit 3-3).

We wrote this casebook on the assumption that employers will continue to play a role in making health insurance coverage decisions, and also assuming that fiscally responsible business will have to continue to put limits on the types and amounts of coverage that they can reasonably and sustainably provide. The ethical question for employers then—given the current system, which puts the onus upon employers for making these decisions—is what kind of process should your business use to decide what insurance coverage option(s) to offer? If your goal is to provide the best possible coverage, at reasonable cost, and with the greatest degree of employee satisfaction, then the Ethical Guideposts should be helpful.

In the following chapters we'll talk about each Ethical Guide-

EXHIBIT 3-3
WHY HAS EMPLOYER-SPONSORED
HEALTH CARE COVERAGE BEEN
SO RESILIENT?

For most of the time that health insurance has been around, the plans have been quite similar. Under fee-for-service, the dominant payment method until the late 1980s and early 1990s, most insurance was essentially the same. But since the advent of managed care, insurance has diversified in offerings and quality—employers and their employees can choose different plans (HMO, PPO) and different types of coverage within plans.

This has led some to suggest that direct-to-consumer insurance is the next step: Instead of having employers serve as mediators and pick which one or few plans to offer, why not have employees choose from a standard smorgasbord of plans?

Perhaps this will occur, but we suspect that employer-sponsored health care will remain important for the foreseeable future for two principal reasons. First, employers are in a better position than individuals to negotiate with health plans for lower costs and better coverage. Second, as you know, the amount of information that must be processed to make an informed decision can be overwhelming for an individual, even if they have special training in assessing coverage options. Many employees already spend an untold number of hours deciding among a limited number of plans—imagine how much more time they would have to spend if the number of options were to increase exponentially. Done right, employers can help their employees weed out options that are not viable and focus on choices that matter most.

post in detail, and sort through dozens of examples where things went wrong and where things went right. First, though, there are a few basic terms that you should be familiar with.

The Basic Terminology of Health Insurance Coverage

Here are simple descriptions of some terms that will come up repeatedly in discussing health insurance coverage.

Annual Enrollment Period: A period of time during which employees and their dependents who have not enrolled in a health insurance plan may do so.

Benefit Schedule: A listing of covered services, often specifying co-payments, deductibles, coinsurance, and specific limitations of a health insurance plan.

Benefits: This can mean the whole package of covered medical services, but it also sometimes refers to the amount of charges that are paid for by the insurance company after the employee's co-payment and/or deductible requirements have been met.

Broker: A person who has obtained a state license to sell and service contracts for health insurance, usually by multiple health plans or insurers. Note that a broker usually makes a commission on sales and so is generally considered to be a salesperson for the insurers rather than a legal agent of the purchaser.

Capitation: A method of paying for health care services on the basis of the number of patients who are covered for specific services over a specified period of time. Basically, it is a payment per person (literally, "by the head"), and is to be distinguished from payment on the basis of the cost or number of services that are actually provided.

Claim: A request for payment of benefits under an insurance contract.

Clinical Practice Guideline: A written document that sets out a standard of care, designed to help physicians make decisions about the most appropriate course of treatment for a specific scenario.

Consolidated Omnibus Budget Reconciliation Act (COBRA): A federal law, passed in 1985, which ensures that employees who leave their jobs can still purchase coverage through their former employer's group plan for eighteen months.

Consumer-Driven Health Plans (CDHP): The movement to set up health care benefits around consumer interests and also to shift more direct responsibility for payment of health insurance premiums to consumers/employees. Also called consumer-centric or consumer-directed plans. The *Health Plans* of CDHP is sometimes interchanged with *Health Care,* to describe a general movement toward more reliance on individuals paying more directly for the care they receive or the insurance plans they select.

Co-payment: The dollar amount that a beneficiary must pay for certain covered services. For example, many plans require patients to pay a certain amount each time they visit a doctor. Sometimes co-payments vary depending on the place treatment is received (co-payments might be higher for an emergency room visit compared to a regular clinic visit, for example) or the service used (co-payments for brand-name drugs might be higher than for generic drugs, for example).

Deductible: For some plans, enrollees must pay a certain dollar amount each year before any insurance coverage begins. The deductible is the amount of covered expenses that must be incurred by the enrollee before benefits become payable by the insurer.

Dependent: A person in the beneficiary's family who is also covered by the insurance plan.

Employee Benefits Consultant: A specialist in employee benefits and insurance who is hired by a purchaser (such as an employer or employer group) to provide advice on a health plan purchase.

Employment Retirement Income Security Act (ERISA): A federal law, enacted in 1974, that defines the fiduciary responsibilities of certain employer-sponsored plans (including pension plans and many health plans). In general, ERISA removed health insurance offered by larger employers from state regulations. These employer-sponsored plans are often referred to as "exempt." (See exhibit 3-1.)

Fee-for-Service (FFS) Payment System: A system under which the insurance plan will either reimburse the group member or pay the provider directly for each covered medical expense after the expense has been incurred.

Health Care Flexible Spending Account (HCFSA): An account with funds set aside to pay for the uncovered or unreimbursed portions of qualified medical costs. All employee contributions to FSAs are made from pretax earnings to encourage employees to set aside money for health care expenses. But most FSAs do not "roll over," meaning if the employee doesn't spend all the money in the FSA each year, it is lost.

Health Maintenance Organizations (HMOs): Originally, HMOs were always "prepaid" or "capitated" insurance plans, but today that is no longer the case. It is now possible to be licensed as an HMO under a variety of different payment structures, though most still involve some degree of financial risk for the providers involved. As a result of this confusion in definitions, many commentators are now trying to avoid using the HMO acronym. A more common term today is MCO, which just stands for Managed Care Organization. This simply acknowledges the lack of clarity, of course, rather than fixing it, but it may be the best we can do for now.

Health Plan Employer Data Information Set (HEDIS®): A constantly evolving set of health plan performance measures, originally designed by employers and health plans but now overseen by the National Committee on Quality Assurance (NCQA). The idea of HEDIS® is to provide health care purchasers with standard information on utilization, financial performance, membership enrollment, and so on for all health plans. Not all health plans collect HEDIS® data, however, nor do they all allow NCQA to report their results to purchasers. Still, the HEDIS® data are very helpful in comparing plans side by side on some important quality and value measures.

Health Reimbursement Accounts (HRAs): Defined contribution accounts set up by and paid by employers for employees to use for health care costs each year (usually it is used toward an employee's *deductible*).

Health Savings Accounts (HSAs): A new health insurance option that generally has two parts. First, it includes a health insurance policy that covers only fairly large health care bills (this is often called a "catastrophic" insurance policy). Second, it includes an investment account into which the employee can contribute money and from which the employee can withdraw money tax-free for medical care. Unused money accumulates with tax-free interest until retirement, at which point the employee can withdraw money for any purpose and pay normal income taxes.

Health Insurance Portability and Accountability Ace of 1996 (HIPAA): A federal law passed in 1996 that allows persons to qualify immediately for comparable health insurance coverage when they change employers. It also creates the authority to require the use of national identification systems for patients, physicians and other providers, and employers (though a national patient identifier system has been strongly resisted so far); and to specify the measures required to protect the security and privacy of personally identifiable health care information. It is often referred to as the "HIPAA Privacy Rule," because of its privacy and confidentiality implications.

High-Deductible Health Plan (HDHP): High-deductible health plans have been recently introduced. In these plans, members pay for all of their own care up to a certain dollar amount each year, often using pretax funds held in a special account (for example, a *health savings account* or a *health reimbursement account*). After reaching the yearly spending limit, or *deductible*, his or her medical costs are largely covered by an insurer.

Indemnity Health Plan: Indemnity health insurance plans are also called fee-for-service (see above). These plans primarily existed before the rise of *HMOs, PPOs*, and the other members of the alphabet soup of *MCOs*. With an indemnity plan, the individual pays a predetermined percentage of the cost for health care services, and the insurance company pays the other percentage. For example, an individual might pay 20 percent for services and the insurance company pays 80 percent.

Managed Care: There seems to be general agreement that "managed care" is "a regrettably nebulous term."[1] In general, managed care refers to any type of health care delivery system that attempts to manage the quality and cost of health care, as well as access to that care, for a defined group of enrolled members.

Managed Care Organization (MCO): See health maintenance organization, above. An MCO can be any organization, entity, or system that uses any of an ever-growing number of techniques to manage the accessibility, cost, and quality of health care. Also known as a *managed care plan*.

Medigap Insurance Policies: Medigap insurance is offered by private insurance companies and is designed to pay for costs that Medicare does not cover.

Ombudsman: An ombudsman receives and responds to questions, concerns, and complaints about any number of plans. He is usually an independent agent who helps insured individuals address questions or concerns with their coverage. In the United States, ombudsmen are often part of the state government.

Personal Care Account (PCA): Funds made available by an employer that employees can use to pay for some or all of their *deductible*.

Preexisting Conditions: A medical condition that is excluded from coverage by an insurance company because the condition was believed to exist prior to the individual's obtaining a policy.

Point-of-Service Plan (POS): Sometimes referred to as a hybrid of an *HMO* and *PPO*, these plans pay for most costs from a preselected physician. Other out-of-network physician visits are allowed, but without a referral from the preselected physician, patients pay for most of the costs of these visits.

Preferred Provider Organizations (PPO): A type of health insurance program (this is another kind of *MCO*, of course) that includes a limited group of physicians and hospitals. Enrollees typically must pay more—sometimes a great deal more, sometimes only a little more—to see physicians or use hospitals that are not part of the PPO network.

Premiums: The amount paid by the employee on a periodic basis for coverage under the insurance contract.

Reasonable and Customary Fees: The average fee charged by a particular type of health care practitioner within a geographic area. The term is often used by medical plans as the amount of money they will approve for a specific test or procedure

Utilization Review: A set of techniques to monitor the use of, or evaluate the clinical necessity, appropriateness, efficacy, or efficiency of health care services, procedures, or settings. Most often, this term is used to refer to a process an MCO might use to decide whether or not to pay for a service. It can occur before the service is delivered (in which case it is called "prospective review" or "precertification") or it can occur after the service is delivered.

Note

1. Peter R. Kongstvedt, *The Managed Health Care Handbook*, 3rd edition (New York: Aspen Publishers. 1996), p. 996.

PART I

The Five Ethical Guideposts of Fair Decision-Making

A Clear Choice

The Decision-Making Process
Should Be *Transparent*

*V*ictor Ong is the executive director of Outdoor Allies, a small
nonprofit with fifty employees that is dedicated to maintaining walking trails in wooded areas around New England.

Every April the Allies sponsor events on and around Earth
Day, including a big day-long concert downtown. This year Victor
was juggling an extra challenge along with the yearly Earth Day
festivities. In an attempt to control rapidly rising health costs, Victor had been working with a benefits consultant who recommended that Outdoor Allies try a high-deductible health plan
instead of the preferred provider organization plan they had been
using for the past few years. By making this switch, employees can
keep using the same doctors and hospitals and the cost of their
premiums will remain almost the same. Only their deductibles will
increase.

Victor wanted to make a decision about the Allies' coverage
quickly so he could focus his time and energy on managing the
Earth Day events. On March 31st, he made the decision to switch
all employees' health coverage to the high-deductible plan, effective April 15th. But then, rather than distract his employees from

their busy April schedule, Victor waited to announce the changes until an all-employee meeting on May 3rd.[1]

When Victor described the health plan change at the May meeting, many employees responded positively. They were generally glad not to see double digit increases in their premiums and happy that they could keep seeing their usual doctors. Kendra Tyson and Julio Suarez, however, were quite upset that they had not been told earlier. They received medical services in April and expected to pay their usual deductible under the preferred provider organization instead of the higher deductible that had just been announced. After the meeting, the two of them spoke to Victor about the possibility of Outdoor Allies reimbursing them for the difference in deductible for the cost of the services they received in April.

Victor now finds himself in a tough spot. He made a health benefits design decision while under time pressure and then was too busy to share that decision with his employees right away. But did Victor make a mistake? Is it really unfair, as Kendra and Julio claim, to ask them to pay a higher deductible than they had planned on? Should Kendra and Julio be reimbursed the difference by their employer?

What if Kendra and Julio, who received health care services under the new plan without knowing it, would have chosen to purchase those services whether or not they would have to pay more for them out-of-pocket? Even so, most people would probably agree that it was unfair that they were not told about a benefits decision that directly affected them until after it was too late for them to do anything about it. A lack of transparency led them to make uninformed health spending decisions—and, maybe more importantly, it led them to become angry with Victor. Especially in such a small employment setting, that anger could become a major problem.

Victor's decision and the way he arrived at it were not transparent to his employees. In this chapter, we'll consider the importance of transparency in health benefits and look at four key ways for employers to ensure that their health care coverage decisions are as transparent as possible.

Ethical Guidepost #1

Transparency: Your employees should understand their health benefits and how decisions are made about changes to their health benefits.

Four Ways to Make **Transparent** Decisions

#1: Communicate clearly and consistently with your employees about health care coverage decisions, using language that is easy to understand.

#2: Explain why there are limits on health care coverage. Tell your employees about the trade-offs that are involved in designing health care packages.

#3: Explain to your employees in writing:

Who is eligible for coverage through your company,

Why your company offers health benefits, and

The types of considerations you take into account as you choose which health plan(s) to offer.

#4 Tell employees how to appeal health care coverage decisions and give them a person they can turn to for assistance with appeals and other questions.

Why Transparency Is Important

Transparency means telling your employees about their health insurance coverage options. But it's more than that. It also means telling them how you came to decide on those options, and why changes are being made when they are. In short, transparency means that your employees know everything they need to know about their health insurance coverage and how it may change over time.

In essence, transparency is a very thorough type of honesty. And, as with honesty, in some cases it can be hard to be fully transparent. But just like being dishonest, making nontransparent decisions can cause serious problems for you and your employees.

With almost every decision about health coverage, the truth will win out in the end. Eventually, employees discover that services aren't covered or that co-payments have increased. And if your employees believe that you haven't been open and honest with them about their health coverage and why it is changing, the consequences can be far worse than simply explaining up front why you are making a tough coverage decision. Lack of transparency can become a bigger problem than the original decision. Remember the old saw that "the cover-up is worse than the crime"? Of course making hard choices about health care coverage is not a crime. And making hard choices is also not unethical. But trying to conceal those decisions from your employees is.

Transparency in health care coverage decisions makes good sense for every employer. For the sake of business stability, it is always best to actively inform employees of decisions that will inevitably affect them, even if you think they'll be unhappy. In fact, it's probably especially important to be transparent about decisions that might make your employees unhappy. They'll be a lot less angry if you are honest with them than if they discover later that you've been hiding something.

Both medically and ethically, transparency is also necessary for employees to make good health care decisions. Employees need to know what they will have to pay for the health care services they get. They may need to discuss alternative medical options with their doctor, depending on what is or is not covered. This can be especially true with some newer health plans, which put more financial responsibilities on patients (see exhibit 4-1). If your employees are going to be held financially accountable for their health

EXHIBIT 4-1
TRANSPARENCY AND
OUT-OF-POCKET EXPENSES

More and more health plans have high deductibles, meaning that employees' out-of-pocket expenses are more directly affected by the costs of the care they receive. When employees are paying for their care directly out of pocket, it's more likely they'll want to shop around for some medical services. If some physicians can do mole removals or hernia repairs or cataract removals for much less than others, this could make a big difference for your employees. Although you can't control how much different physicians and providers charge, you can help your employees a great deal by finding and distributing materials that compare the costs of health care in the area. Bear in mind, however, that cheaper isn't always better. It is also important to provide information about the quality of care when you can (see chapter 7, on the Ethical Guidepost, *Sensitive to Value*).

care decisions, they deserve to know this before they are asked to make health care choices.

Transparency Is Critical in Times of Transition

Many employees assume that their health plan will stay the same from year to year unless they decide to make changes themselves. But this is not always the case. And, as you know, not all health insurance plans are the same.

In particular, employers in the United States are increasingly offering their employees high-deductible, so-called "consumer-driven," coverage options, such as the plan offered by Outdoor

Allies in the case above. These plans come in many forms (see exhibit 4-2). Many involve employees covering their own health care with pretax dollars until their expenditures reach a preset deductible, the size of which varies with the employer and the plan. When an employee reaches this deductible, his or her coverage shifts to a more traditional health insurance model, such as a preferred provider organization (PPO), in which most or all care costs are covered by the insurer. These plans represent a major change from traditional HMOs and PPOs; services that were covered under those models must, in the new plans, be paid for by the

EXHIBIT 4-2
THE INSURANCE CHANGE
THAT VICTOR MADE

In a preferred provider organization, members get discounted services from a network of providers and receive partial coverage for seeing out-of-network providers. Deductibles are usually modest as long as the employee is using in-network providers. (See the glossary in chapter 3 for more information.)

In high-deductible health plans, members pay for all of their own care up to a certain dollar amount each year, often using pretax funds held in a special account. After a member reaches the yearly spending limit, or deductible, his or her medical costs are largely covered by an insurer. Some services may be covered even before a member reaches the deductible, however. There are many different kinds of high-deductible health plans, with different size deductibles and amounts, if any, that the employer contributes to the pretax fund, among other features.

insured individual until he or she reaches the higher deductible (see exhibit 4-3).

Transparency is especially important when businesses are making changes to their coverage. Changing to a different type of plan altogether, such as changing from traditional health insurance to a high-deductible plan, or from an HMO-type plan to a PPO-type plan, can be especially confusing for employees who have gotten used to the old plan. But even a simple change in covered benefits, such as removing coverage for vision care, should be made transparent.

To be transparent about changes, businesses need to take into account the likely assumptions their employees will make about their health coverage, including the assumption that any new

EXHIBIT 4-3
THE LINK BETWEEN
"CONSUMER-DRIVEN" AND
"HIGH-DEDUCTIBLE"
HEALTH PLANS

"Consumer-driven" health coverage is coverage that allows enrollees to customize their health care benefits packages by choosing among a number of benefits possibilities through various providers. While you can probably imagine a lot of different ways for options to be presented to make a benefits package "consumer-driven," in reality today, "consumer-driven" health coverage almost always consists of a high-deductible health plan. These plans are then usually coupled with a "health savings account," which allows the employee to use pretax dollars for certain health care purchases. Recently, it has become possible to carry the value of these accounts over from year to year.

health plan will operate essentially like the old one. Whether your business is changing to a high-deductible plan or just changing the covered benefits of your preferred provider organization, you should *provide your employees with a side-by-side comparison of the new plan and the old plan.* This can help employees to see and understand any significant changes in coverage. Sometimes this simple step alone can make a change in coverage very clear.

In many cases, health plans themselves will provide information about what services they cover. These materials, like brochures or one-page summaries, can be very helpful for explaining the plan. But remember that your employees might need to spend a good deal of time trying to understand a new plan. If you helped to make the decision to switch to a new plan, then you will probably be an expert on the new plan compared to your employees. And you are probably the only one who can really explain *why* you are making the change. So it is up to you to give your employees clear information on the new plan *and* on the reasons why the change is being made.

You might be thinking, "Isn't it unfair to ask employers to make sure their employees understand new or changing health plans?"

Let's be transparent about what the expectation for transparency is. Of course you cannot force an employee to understand the health plan. But you also can't just assume that your employees will figure out changes in the health plan that you had to study in depth, perhaps for weeks, before you decided on them. What you can and should do, therefore, is offer information about any changes in ways that your employees are most likely to understand. You can also make sure they have someone they can turn to with questions.

As the insurance industry continues to evolve, your employees will have to keep learning about new types of health plans just like you are. In some cases, newer health plans can seem like they work in ways that are exactly the opposite of health plans they are most familiar with! This makes clear communication about new plans, or any other changes, even more important.

Transparency and Communication Barriers

Transparency is about helping your employees understand the benefits decisions that affect them. If your employee population includes people who communicate more easily in languages other than English, it can be well worth it to have information professionally translated. You can use the 5/50 rule as a rough guide. If more than 5 percent of your employees, or more than 50 employees in total, have a non-English language as their primary language, you should have the information translated. Of course, in some cases even a single person might need an interpreter to help make decisions about health care, so each business will have to evaluate this need individually.

Keep in mind also that communicating across cultures means more than just using the right language. You should be aware of other cultural barriers that some employees might encounter in learning about health care coverage. For example, if a large percentage of your employees are immigrants or are otherwise unfamiliar with the employer-based insurance system in the United States, information might need to be shaped accordingly.

In addition to language and culture, there are several other common barriers to effective communication.[2] If you know that your employees have limited literacy or are otherwise unlikely to be able to understand typical information about health coverage, you will need to address these issues. Information should be accessible to all employees. For example, an online newsletter might be a perfect mode of communication for many employees of a high-tech firm, but it won't be very effective if most of your employees don't have Internet access.

Why Wouldn't an Employer Be Transparent?

In the course of interviews with many business leaders from around the country, we've come across two common reasons why some employers have chosen not to be fully open with their employees about their health care coverage decisions. Sometimes they are more comfortable making sure employees understand *what is* covered and *what is not* covered and less comfortable sharing the reasons *why* this is so. But since both are important, let's talk about both.

1. *"It's not practical to inform all employees about all the health benefits decisions that affect them. It would be a full-time job for each employee to read all of those documents."*

Even in a small business, it can be hard to get all health benefits–related information to all employees. In a very large organization, it can be a fool's errand. Between the decisions that you make, the decisions that the health plans you contract with make, and all the state and federal regulations that can affect coverage, there is simply too much information for any one employee to absorb. In short, the degree of your transparency about these issues is likely to be limited by some key resources: namely, *time* and *money*. Instead of aiming for an exhaustive communication strategy, it can be more effective to focus on getting out information about basic features. Usually this can be done with a side-by-side table, especially when a change is being made. Comparing coverage side-by-side gives employees the opportunity to see how their coverage will change, without being overwhelmed. Then, more detailed information should be available for those who want it, perhaps on a Web site, and a person should be named who can answer additional questions.

2. *"If employees get to see the process, they'll want to control it, and will demand a more active role."*

Some business owners and human resources professionals fear that employees will ask for or expect more extensive and expensive coverage if they are allowed to peek into the process for choosing coverage. But on the contrary, many experts now believe that if employees are more aware of the costs and trade-offs involved in making health care coverage decisions, they will actually demand less. At the very least, they will appreciate why their employers cannot provide coverage without limits. Choosing health care coverage means making tough choices. In fact, economists have shown that the costs of health care coverage, in one way or another, eventually come straight out of employees' wages. Employees need to understand this. If they don't, then they are even more likely to believe the decisions are unfair.

If you really are afraid to tell your employees how you pick health insurance coverage and why you picked the coverage you did, your first step should be to review your existing processes to see how they can be improved. Most of the time, these decision processes are pretty straightforward and there is no reason to conceal them from employees. But if, after this review, you would still be embarrassed to admit to your employees how you make these decisions, then your process should probably be revamped. After all, at some point your embarrassing decisions might come to light in a newspaper story.

Maximizing the Transparency of Your Decision-Making

Share Responsibilities

Be clear about who has responsibility for communicating particular elements of your benefits design to your employees. For example, some or all of your employees may be covered by an HMO. If the HMO will cover additional services, or exclude services, during the new contract year, be clear about which organization (you, the HMO, or another party) is responsible for notifying your employees of the changes and the reasons for any changes. Then make sure it really happens.

It is also important for your organization to take responsibility for its decisions, even if you delegate the job of communicating those decisions to others. While some decisions are forced by changes in health plan offerings or by regulations, businesses make many choices about the amount and type of coverage they purchase and offer to employees. This is especially true for self-insured employers who design their own health coverage plans. Although you may arrange for your health plan to inform your employees about your benefits design decisions (for example, an increased emergency room co-payment), it is not fair to have employees "shoot the messenger," or blame the health plan for a coverage decision they dislike, simply because the health plan first communicated it to them. For self-insured employers, most decisions about changing benefits are made as a compromise during negotiations between the employer and the plan—and that's how they should be presented to your employees.

Prioritize and Demystify

It is much more important and realistic for your employees to understand how decisions are made and how new services are evaluated than for every employee to know every time a new drug is covered or a preliminary meeting is held with a new benefits consultant to consider changes to the plans. At a minimum, employees should understand the roles that different decision-makers play in shaping their coverage. And they should know something about the rational basis for these decisions (such as the principles, objectives, and sources of information used in making the decisions). Do you simply pick covered services out of a hat? Of course not. But your employees might think you do if they are not given any better idea of how you make coverage decisions. Do you consult with an insurance broker? Do you work with a consultant? Do you compare your offerings to what other businesses offer? Did you look at cost-effectiveness studies to evaluate a new therapy for coverage? Those are the sorts of things that you can tell your employees. They can demystify the process and improve your employees' understanding and, hopefully, their trust in you.

Prioritizing information about how decisions are made and demystifying the process for your employees is important so that employees can feel empowered to use their coverage responsibly. It also allows them to address their questions and concerns to the appropriate people and organizations.

What's the Business Case for Transparency?

By attending to transparency, you can foster employee morale, improve relations between employees and management, gain employee understanding of the tough choices and trade-offs that have to be made, and avoid costly misunderstandings about coverage. You might even lower your overall health coverage costs.

- It might be better to be transparent than it is to spend more! Benefits transparency improves employee retention even more than increasing the dollar amount spent on benefits. A 2004 Watson Wyatt World@Work Study™ found that 22 percent of employees at organizations that fund rich benefit packages but fail to communicate their value are satisfied with their benefits. On the other hand, among employees of organizations that effectively communicate the value of *less* rich benefit packages, 76 percent of employees are satisfied with their benefits.[3]

- When employees understand the health coverage processes that affect them, they will feel a greater sense of control over their health care, which can positively affect morale, health status, and productivity in turn.

- Misunderstandings arise when employees do not understand how health benefits decisions are made and what coverage limits they face. Avoid employee anger and frustration, and avoid spending the time and money it takes to resolve these situations, by being transparent about your decisions in the first place.

- Effective communication helps employees appreciate their "hidden paycheck," that is, the value of the nonsalary employment benefits they receive. When employees realize how much is spent by employers on their health care, they are more likely to understand when changes or limits in coverage may be necessary for the company's solvency and their continued employment.

- By being transparent about benefits decisions when your company is doing well financially, you build trust and credibility with your employees. If you've built a foundation of trust and openness, your employees will be more likely to believe you and respect your decisions if you must make benefits cuts during leaner times.

Transparency as the Foundation of Fairness

As you proceed through this book and develop a strategy for fair health benefits decision-making, bear in mind that the other four Ethical Guideposts all rely on the transparency of your coverage decision-making process. Each of the five benchmarks is equally important, but transparency lays the foundation for the others. Without delving too deeply into the later chapters, let's consider why this is so.

(1) *Participatory:* In chapter 5, we'll look at the importance of involving your employees in processes for designing and administering health benefits. Employees must understand the processes they are contributing to if they are to participate meaningfully.

(2) *Consistent:* In chapter 6, we'll explore how consistent, equitable decision-making contributes to the overall fairness

of health coverage decisions. For your employees to understand that your decisions are consistent, they must understand the decisions and also the decision-making process. If you are clear with them about the details of their own health plans, but do not achieve transparency about the overall decision-making processes and rationales, they will lack the context to assess and appreciate your efforts to be consistent.

(3) *Sensitive to Value:* In chapter 7, we'll consider how designing coverage decision procedures that are sensitive to value contributes to fairness. Being sensitive to value means working with the resources you have to get the most effective and efficient health care you can for your employees. The studies and strategies used to determine what health care coverage is most cost-effective are sometimes complicated and controversial. Transparency about what information is being used to determine that a service is worth covering or not is critical. The only way for employees to understand and respect the decisions that are made is if they know about the information sources and criteria that employers and others use to decide what services will be covered. If you're sensitive to value but not transparent about your approach, your decisions might appear to your employees to be arbitrary or self-serving.

(4) *Compassionate:* In chapter 8, we'll look at the importance of handling your organization's health benefits in ways that are responsive to the needs of especially vulnerable individuals or those with special needs. It is crucial that your organization's approach to the special needs of those who are injured and ill be transparent to your employees. Each employee has the potential to become critically ill or to develop special health care needs. When you are clear about your approach to unusual or extremely expensive health needs, you address a concern that is salient to all

your employees, regardless of their current health status or ability to navigate the health care system. Also, even the most well-funded health plan must at some point limit its flexibility, and compassion cannot be expressed by financing every health care–related request. Being straightforward and honest with your employees about these issues, particularly in calm, noncrisis situations, can lay the foundation for productive and effective collaboration when health crises and other challenges arise.

Case Studies

The five cases in this chapter illustrate how some employers have managed to be transparent in their health care coverage decisions. Some of these cases may seem very similar to your own situation; others may involve details that just do not apply to your circumstances. Each case, and the short discussion that follows, is meant to illustrate one or more of the steps in achieving transparency, while also showing how transparency can bolster your company's reputation for fairness as well as your bottom line.

Case 1: Using Clear Language

It had been an emotional morning in the human resources department of the Paper Chase Office Supply Company. Saul from distributions stormed in, angry and wanting answers. His wife was undergoing chemotherapy for cancer and had recently lost her hair. She was quite upset about it, but her mood had improved when she began looking at wig catalogs. When Saul called his health insurance company to see if there was a wig manufacturer they recommended, a plan representative told him that wigs were not covered by his plan.

Saul and his wife found this ridiculous. Losing your hair is part of cancer treatment! Shouldn't the treatment for that problem

*be covered? They searched Saul's health coverage documents for
an explanation and didn't find a word about wigs.*

*Saul had two bones to pick with human resources. First, he
wanted to know why wigs weren't covered, and second, if they
weren't covered, why didn't it say so in his coverage documents?
Someone in human resources had handled this problem before,
and she pointed out a line in the "exclusions" section of Saul's
coverage description. "Cranial prostheses" were not covered by
Saul's health plan, and cranial prostheses are wigs. Saul sighed
heavily.*

The first lesson we can take from Saul's case is obvious: Avoid
jargon! The most comprehensive benefits documentation in the
world is not worth much if only an expert on medicine or health
insurance can figure it out. In addition to the documents you produce, consider how coverage limits and their rationales are described in the documents that your employees receive from the
health plans you contract with.

Some readers might think that Saul's wife's wig should be covered by Paper Chase's insurance; others might not. We are not
arguing for or against coverage here; rather, we want to make a
case for clear and thorough communication about limits, and not
just once a problem arises.

Let's put Saul's experience in context. If his coverage has been
explained clearly all along, and he generally feels that Paper Chase
is on his side, he might be willing to consider why his employer
and his insurers make the benefits design choices they do. He
might even come to agree with them. But if this coverage limit is
just one in a line of confusing or, in his opinion, unjustified coverage decisions, Saul will be considerably less open to working
calmly with Paper Chase and his health plan to resolve the matter.

Finally, consider this statistic, noted earlier in our business case
for transparency. A 2004 Watson Wyatt World@Work Study
found that "only 22 percent of employees at organizations that
poorly communicate the value of their rich benefit programs are

satisfied with their benefit package[, while] 76 percent of employees at organizations that effectively communicate the value of less rich benefit packages are satisfied."[4]

"Less rich benefit packages" are those that, by definition, place greater limitations upon coverage. This study suggests that by effectively communicating these limits, employers are able to reap one of the central employer benefits of providing health care coverage (that is, a satisfied work force) even without providing a "rich benefit package." We are not suggesting that you attempt to replace a rich health coverage package with very thorough communication about narrower benefits. However, you should consider that failing to be transparent about benefits limits may effectively *lower* the value of the benefits you do provide, in terms of the effect of those benefits on employee satisfaction and retention.

Case 2: Acknowledge Limits

It had not been a very profitable year for Grocery Giant, a large regional retail grocer. Rumors swirled among employees about pay cuts and downsizing. No one was looking forward to the upcoming open enrollment meeting where changes in the company's health plans would be announced.

Grocery Giant's CEO, Jacqueline Vasquez, had been working with benefits consultants to develop a presentation on the coming changes in health coverage options. In response to the chain's rapidly rising health costs and stagnant profits, they had developed a set of health plans which would increase the amount of money employees had to contribute to their own health coverage, among other changes.

Jacqueline wanted to inform employees about the changes without fostering resentment toward the company, a flood of complaints to human resources, and a plunge in morale. She and her human resources team decided on an honest and forthright approach. At mandatory employee meetings, and in information packets distributed in Spanish and English, Grocery Giant man-

agement explained to their employees how much health costs had increased. Using diagrams and citing figures, they compared what the company had been paying for health care with the amount employees had been contributing.

At each meeting, some employees gasped when they heard how much the company had been contributing to their health coverage. Many had been genuinely unaware that health insurance cost so much. They had only been paying attention to what was taken out of their paychecks for premiums and what they were paying in co-pays.

The presenters concluded the meeting with a diagram that showed how Grocery Giant hoped to save several stores and improve the distribution network by reinvesting the money it would save by increasing employee contributions to health care coverage. They also showed projections of improved company profits if they were able to make these changes. They emphasized that the company did not plan to eliminate coverage. But they wanted employees to fully understand how significant health care costs were to the overall business plan.

Having provided their employees with some background on the true cost of health coverage and its impact on the company's solvency, the presenters began to describe the new health plan options that would be offered to Grocery Giant employees during open enrollment.

Grocery Giant was honest with its employees about the real costs of health care. The company's openness contributed to its success at limiting health insurance premium increases to 6 percent in 2005, when average premiums for employer-sponsored insurance rose by 11.2 percent.

These weren't one-time savings either. In 2006 Grocery Giant expects a 5 percent cost increase for health coverage, compared to its competitors' projected 10–11 percent hike.

Studies have shown that employees are largely unaware of what their employers pay for their health care benefits. Employees tend to overestimate what they pay toward their health coverage and drastically underestimate their employer's contribution.[5]

The real costs of health coverage and your organization's real financial constraints and objectives should be transparent to your employees. If they are not, health benefits cuts will rankle, both because no one likes to hear about health care limits and because your employees don't think you are paying as much as you are. For your benefits package to be valuable to your organization, in terms of employee retention, recruitment, and morale, you must effectively communicate to employees how much you're investing in their health care.

In the absence of real information about coverage decisions, employees tend to assume that dollars saved on their health care will benefit someone other than themselves. For more on this possibility, see case 4 below. If you want employees to trust you when you talk about financial constraints that limit their coverage, you must make ongoing efforts to maintain transparency about your health coverage decision-making.

Case 3: Tell Employees Who, What, Where, *and* Why

Jim Green, the owner of Babyblue Children's Clothing Company, with roughly 1,500 employees, is well known in his community. He's on the board of a number of local organizations that raise money for research on childhood illnesses.

Rachel Smith had been working at Babyblue for about five years when her son was diagnosed with asthma. She had been satisfied with her health coverage, but after her son's diagnosis she was overwhelmed with out-of-pocket costs associated with his preventive prescriptions. If she only filled the prescription for his inhaler, she could save some money. But it wasn't worth it for her to watch her son suffer through the attacks. Her plan required particularly high coinsurance for brand-name drugs, and there were no generic equivalents for the preventive medications.[6] She had no choice but to buy the brand-name product.

Rachel tried to get some assistance or explanation from her health plan, but no one she could reach was very helpful. She began to talk to her co-workers about her health cost woes, and speculated openly that Jim had designed a plan that offered more generous coverage for the diseases he did fundraising for, and less for others. A few employees scoffed at this idea, but others grumbled along with her.

When human resources caught wind of Rachel's accusation, they found it ridiculous. Jim had very little to do with the decisions they made about the health insurance coverage they offered to employees. Babyblue had contracted with a benefits consulting firm to design the plan. Jim had signed off on the final plan, but had not had any input on the specific diseases or treatments that would get coverage.

Though they sympathized with Rachel's difficult situation, staff members in Babyblue's human resources department sorely wished she had spoken to them first. They might have been able to help her get some answers, and maybe even better coverage for her son's prescriptions. Instead, they were now busy quelling rumors and handling employee discontent.

This case demonstrates an unfortunate chain of events. At a number of points, more transparent health benefits decision-making procedures could have produced better outcomes for Rachel's peace of mind, for Babyblue's bottom line, and even for Rachel's son's health.

If Rachel had been well informed about how health benefits design decisions are made at Babyblue, she would not have accused the owner, Jim Green, of demonstrating bias in the company's coverage. It is essential that employees understand who is involved and what types of considerations come into play as well as what is covered and what isn't. Rumors will tend to rush in to fill any information gaps you leave. In other words, if you don't give your employees accurate information about the way coverage decisions are made, they are likely to develop their own interpretation and share it with others.

It's also key for employees to understand the main goals of your company's health coverage. Rachel's troubles stemmed from the fact that her coverage through Babyblue left her with very high co-pays for a brand-name prescription for her son, for which there was no generic equivalent. It is unlikely that the benefits design decision that created this situation was intended to penalize children with asthma. It might have been intended to promote efficient use of limited funds, which could be a rationale that Rachel would generally support. If Rachel understood the company's goals with respect to coverage, as well as the financial constraints under which the benefits design decisions were made (see Goal #1), she might have responded differently.

In short, make sure your employees understand:

WHO is involved in making health care coverage decisions?

WHAT gets covered under your health plan?

WHERE decisions are made: at what levels of your organization and at which other organizations?

WHY decisions are made as they are: what criteria do decisions rest upon?

When a problem does arise, try to see it as an instructional moment for your company. Without violating individual employees' privacy, consider addressing misunderstandings about benefits design processes in meetings or in writing. See case 5 below for some further steps that could be taken to prevent a situation like this.

Case 4: Explain Trade-Offs

Health benefits changes were afoot at the midsize Web site development firm Intelligent Design (ID), and all options called for em-

ployees' assuming a larger share of their health care costs. ID's co-CEOs, Talia and Marc Cooper, wanted their employees to understand why their health costs were rising. Though benefits consultants had addressed employees' questions at open enrollment meetings, the Coopers got the impression that some employees still thought that individual ID managers were benefiting from the cuts in ID's share of the benefits cost. They overheard one complaint about new cars in management's parking spots.

Talia and Marc published the following letter in the company's online newsletter to respond to employee concerns.

"You've all heard about your personal health coverage costs rising in the coming year. We weren't happy about increasing your contribution, but we had to do it. The numbers speak for themselves. We could have covered cost-of-living raises and continued paying for last year's share of your health coverage if we had:

A) Drastically reduced family coverage.

-OR-

B) Moved forty-five employees to part-time, nonbenefit-earning positions.

-OR-

C) Postponed 50 percent of essential software upgrades for at least one year.

Let's be brutally honest. Some of you may be wondering about our own salaries. Our take-home pay, just like yours, is one of the costs of doing business that we must consider when we make budget decisions. This includes decisions about health care coverage. But have these cuts in health benefits been done to pad our wallets?

The answer is no. Because we are reducing benefits, we have also given ourselves only cost-of-living raises this year. Your increased out-of-pocket health care spending is not funding our vacations or upgrades for our home computers. To put *it simply, health costs are up, and in order to maintain thorough coverage for all employees and their families, we had to share more costs with you. Please feel free, as always, to share any questions or concerns you may have with us or with anyone in the Human Resources office."*

Talia and Marc weren't sure if they should be so blunt with their employees. Still, they thought that laying all their cards on the table might work to their advantage.

From a budgeting perspective, a dollar spent on health care cannot be spent on anything else. If you spend a dollar on health care coverage for your employees, you can't apply it to salary increases, capital improvements, employee pensions, and so on.

Here's the catch. When it comes to making coverage decisions, it might be tempting to talk to your employees about health coverage as if health care is your organization's number one priority. At certain times—say, when you are confronted with someone who is sick and unsatisfied with the coverage—you might even feel that it should be that important. But health care coverage costs must be balanced against the rest of your business's financial priorities (see exhibit 4-4). You know that (or you wouldn't still be in business!), and it is important that your employees understand it too.

You consider a number of legitimate uses for every dollar your organization spends. While you may see these choices as balancing obligations and weighing priorities, it is possible that your employees will see conflicts of interest depending on your perceived role as a decision-maker. In the case above, rumors circulated about the Coopers because employees perceived a conflict between their interest in their own financial well-being and their interest in funding health coverage for their employees.

By now you shouldn't be surprised to hear that transparency can help you resolve these tensions and stop them from arising in the first place. The need to make trade-offs among various business expenses is not going to go away, and, given the rising cost of health care coverage, the decisions will probably only get harder.

EXHIBIT 4-4
WHAT IS AT STAKE IN HEALTH
COVERAGE TRADE-OFFS?

- 29 percent of human resources professionals say high health care costs are spurring cuts in other employee benefits

- 28 percent expect hiring cuts

- 22 percent expect to reduce employee salaries and raises

- 19 percent expect less employee training and professional development

- 12 percent expect fewer technology investments

Source: "Survey by the Society for Human Resource Management," December 2004.

Therefore, maintaining positive relations with your employees, even in the face of health care cuts, depends on acknowledging that you, as a decision-maker, face conflicting obligations and on explaining how these challenging decisions are made.

If your employees worry about someone else getting personal financial gain from decisions that decrease their coverage, you should speak directly to those concerns. Obfuscation will only lead to more resentment. In some cases, there will be a good reason for improving the financial situation of a business owner or CEO even in the face of benefit cuts for the employees. Especially in smaller businesses, so long as employees can understand the business leader's significance to the success of this business, it will be possible to explain what is happening. For larger businesses, decisions about executive salaries and decisions about health insurance coverage will be made in very different contexts, often by different people at different levels of your organization. Regardless of how your health care coverage decisions are made, be sure that you explain the process as clearly as possible.

Acknowledge the many demands on resources and decision-makers' conflicting obligations to avoid rumors and resentment. It may seem distasteful to talk about health coverage costs in the same breath as, for example, the cost of expanding the employee parking lot. But your employees won't appreciate the difficult decisions you face, or the fact that you don't personally benefit from cutting their coverage, unless you make your process and your reasons explicit to them.

Case 5: Knowing Where to Turn for Help

Imagine how things might have turned out differently for Baby-blue Children's Clothing Company, profiled in case 3 above.

Jim Green, the owner of Babyblue Children's Clothing Company, is well known in his community. He's on the board of a number of local organizations that raise money for research on childhood illnesses.

Rachel Smith had been working at Babyblue for about five years when her son was diagnosed with asthma. She had been satisfied with her health coverage, but after her son's diagnosis she was overwhelmed with out-of-pocket costs associated with his prescriptions. Her plan required particularly high coinsurance for brand-name drugs, but there were no generic equivalents for his preventive medication.[7] She had no choice but to buy the brand-name product.

The Difference

Rachel was very concerned about her financial situation, and she hadn't gotten much help from calling the customer service number on her health insurance card. But she knew there was someone in human resources who was in charge of answering questions and handling problems with health benefits.

In fact, Babyblue had a benefits professional who specialized in health coverage issues. Her name was Olivia Lee, and a receptionist pointed Rachel right to her desk when she walked into the human resources office. Olivia could not personally resolve Rachel's problem, but she had spoken with the ombudsman at Rachel's plan in the past and so she was able to guide Rachel through the plan's appeals process.

A week later, when one of Rachel's coworkers mentioned a problem he was having with his insurance, Rachel told him about Olivia's assistance. Rachel was still in the midst of her health plan's appeals process to get more coverage for her son's prescriptions, and no outcome was guaranteed. Still, she felt positive about her prospects because she did not feel that she was facing her challenge alone.

In case 3, Rachel did not get her concerns resolved. Instead, she ended up spreading rumors that decreased morale and endangered relations between Babyblue's owner and his employees. Clearly, this version shows the better alternative.

Whether you have a full-time benefits staff or you are the owner of a small company with a full plate of responsibilities, only one of which is health benefits, your employees need to know where to go in your organization for help in answering questions or resolving problems they might have with their health coverage (see exhibit 4-5).

Your employees should know that starting an appeal is no guarantee that they will get the coverage they want. But they should also know that coming to you for help is an option. What's most important in terms of transparency is that your employees understand the decisions that affect them and that they understand how to challenge decisions if they think they are incorrect or unfair.

Your role in facilitating your employees' access to an appeals process will vary with your coverage type, organization size, and resources, but, at minimum, you must know the person to contact

EXHIBIT 4-5
WHAT IS AN OMBUDSMAN?

An ombudsman receives and responds to questions, concerns, and complaints about health plans. For more information on plan ombudsmen, see the glossary at the end of chapter 3.

at your employees' health plans when questions arise about coverage. If you don't know, or at least have this information available, employee confusion can quickly escalate into resentment and anger. It can also fuel employees' feelings of powerlessness with respect to their health and health coverage, which could make them less trusting of information you try to send out in the future.

Conclusion

You and your employees benefit when you are transparent about how and why you make decisions about health care coverage. By being clear and honest with your employees about their coverage, even when that means sharing bad news, you fill an information void. If you don't fill that void, rumors and misinformation will, and that's not in anyone's best interest.

Notes

1. Although the legal requirements on disclosure are not always clear, there is a growing body of case law suggesting that employers have a responsibility to inform employees before the date a switch in health coverage becomes effective. The requirement to disclose will depend on state laws and possibly also the

type of insurance or health plan you are choosing and the type of change under consideration.

2. The Ethical Force Program, "Improving communication—improving care: how health care organizations can ensure effective, patient-centered communication with people from diverse populations." American Medical Association, Chicago, IL, 2006.

3. "Communication helps retain top workers," *Financial Executive*, 21(3): April 2005; 12 [no author listed].

4. Ibid.

5. Schauer, quoted in Wojcik, J., "Benefit education, communication needed," *Business Insurance*, 37(8): Feb. 24, 2003; T3

6. http://www.keepkidshealthy.com/inside_pediatrics/saving_money_prescriptions.html.

7. Ibid.

▲

Get It Together

The Decision-Making Process
Should Be Participatory

*I*f Joseph Woo hears one more complaint about his company's
current health plan co-pays or deductibles, he'll snap. Joseph is
*in charge of plan selection for his small company (200 employees),
and he honestly thought the current plan would be a hit. When he
decided to make the change to the current plan, he did it because
the premiums were quite low, giving every employee more take-
home pay each month. The trade-off was that the plan also had
somewhat higher co-pays and deductibles. He thought that more
take-home pay would be a popular change. And yet, employee
complaints about the high deductibles and co-pays piled up.*

*Thankfully, the year is almost up. Joseph has chosen a new
plan with lower co-pays and lower deductibles with only a slightly
higher premium. The trade-off now is that the plan is not as rich
as the prior plan—several items are not covered by the new plan
that the old plan would have covered. Given his recent experiences
with complaints about deductibles and co-payments, he has now
braced for complaints about the higher premiums by preparing*

and distributing a table that compares the different plans' premiums, co-pays, and deductibles.

A couple of weeks after Joseph announces the switch in plans, Mary Lefko, an administrative assistant, is waiting by his office when he arrives at work. She looks upset. When Joseph invites her into his office, she explains that the immunizations for her daughter (born six months ago) were covered by the old plan, but are not covered by the new plan. She knows she would have paid a higher deductible under the old plan, but now she is paying the higher premium and she has to pay for her daughter's immunizations, and she hasn't even begun to meet the current year's deductible. This is particularly difficult because the cost of the vaccinations won't even count toward the deductible. She's not sure where she'll get the money or what she should have done to avoid this situation.

As he had predicted, Joseph is starting to get a new batch of complaints. But this complaint is not what he had prepared for. He picked the new plan according to what he thought employees wanted. He was attentive to his employees' complaints and altered the benefits accordingly to reduce the co-payments and deductibles. But sensitivity to employee complaints isn't enough, if it's not matched with organized efforts to gather employee input. By responding only to complaints, Joseph ends up ignoring any employees who didn't complain and any issues that weren't the subject of a complaint. Some employees may have liked the old plan, and others may have had different complaints, but Joseph never found out because he never asked.

Joseph tried to make a good decision for his employees, but he needed information that was only available through direct participation in the decision-making process by his employees. In this chapter, we'll look at the value of employee participation in health care benefits decisions, and set four specific priorities for meaningful participation.

Ethical Guidepost #2

Participatory: Your employees should have the opportunity to provide input into the decision-making process about their health benefits.

Four Ways to Make **Participatory** Decisions

#1: Include employees on committees that design health benefits packages or that set general coverage rules.

#2: Provide all employees with ample opportunity to give input to those charged with designing their health benefits.

#3: Proactively gather information about your employees' health benefits needs, values, and priorities.

#4: Use the information you gather about your employees' needs, values, and priorities to shape your benefits design decisions.

Joseph wanted to respond to his employees' needs, but he didn't systematically collect input from them. Taking complaints seriously as they arose was a good first step, but Joseph should have actively pursued their opinions and concerns, and he should have done this *before* making his final decisions (see exhibit 5-1). A company the size of his might not have a committee to design benefits, but he could still gather the needed information from his employees. In the end, his employees' participation might have led Joseph to pick the same plan, but, even so, as he now realizes, getting their input in advance would have provided him with an opportunity to deal with Mary's concern and the concerns of the rest of his staff.

Improving Decision-Making Through Employee Participation

You shouldn't be surprised if you think it's intuitively obvious that including employee participation is a nice ideal. Including employ-

EXHIBIT 5-1
FORMAL VERSUS
INFORMAL PARTICIPATION

Informal participation of employees in decision-making—such as hallway conversations or your recollection of employee complaints—can be an important trigger for further investigation. But this kind of participation relies too heavily on the ability to remember and balance all the issues raised. Formal participation—such as by working on a committee, being part of a focus group, or responding to a survey—is important because it leaves a paper trail, reminding you (and your employees) about their contributions to the process. Formal participation has the added advantage of being more transparent to employees.

ees in the decision-making process appeals to our democratic sensibilities. Because health insurance coverage affects the lives and happiness of employees and their families, it's natural to think they should be part of the decision-making process. But employee participation does more than appeal to our democratic ideals, it also improves the credibility and the quality of health care coverage decisions.

Credibility

Employee participation improves the credibility of the decision-making process and of the final decision. Because formal participation provides employees with a clear route to provide input into the process, it gives them the opportunity to understand how the final benefits design reflects their own input. And, in conjunction with transparency, it allows them to understand how these decisions also reflect the input of other employees. So getting meaningful contributions from employees lends credibility both to the process of choosing a plan and to the plan itself.

On the flip side, employees who have no way to participate are more likely to view the problems and difficulties of any benefits package as *your* responsibility, not theirs. Without their participation, the plan is something they must simply endure. Ultimately, this may lead employees to consider other jobs with benefits better suited to their needs. In Joseph's case, he failed to proactively seek input from all of his employees, so that only employees who complained were involved in the process. Because Joseph failed to get input from employees like Mary Lefko, he cannot give Mary a reasonable explanation of how her experience of the costs and benefits of different services was taken into account in planning the new package (see exhibit 5-2).

Quality

The best health care coverage meets your employees' needs efficiently. Employee participation will improve the quality of health care coverage decisions by making clear what your employees' needs are and by improving the efficiency of the benefits in meeting those needs. Without employee input, unnecessary services might be included while real needs might go uncovered.

Not only can employee needs be more accurately identified through participation, but these needs can also be appropriately weighted. Imagine if you opted to extend coverage for one set of procedures because of one person's complaint? That might be the right thing to do, but you wouldn't know if that person is alone in his complaint of if he represents a larger group of employees. If, instead of relying on one person's (or even a group of people's) complaint, you gather input from all your employees, you won't be left in the dark about what your employees need and want and how many of them need or want it.

In the case that started this chapter, if Joseph had gathered employee input about the most important covered benefits, he

EXHIBIT 5-2
SHARE THE COST,
BUT ALSO SHARE THE CONTROL

Let's be very blunt—most of the recent changes in health insurance coverage have probably been pretty negative from your employees' point of view. And future changes probably won't be any more welcome. As increasing costs are no longer sustainable, employers are generally shifting more direct costs to employees, through things like increasing co-pays, deductibles, premiums, and so on. These "cost-sharing" steps are often necessary for employers. This isn't your fault, and your employees should recognize that. But at the same time, you should recognize that your employees are being required to spend more time making decisions about their health care, which can sometimes leave them feeling as though they are gambling with their health. By being involved in the process of picking the health plans they are offered, they are more likely to understand and accept the reasons for these shifts, and as a result, they are more likely to be satisfied with the coverage they eventually get.

might have avoided Mary Lefko's difficult position, perhaps at minimal cost. Of course, it might also have turned out that the best decision was the one he made, but without employee input, Joseph cannot be confident of that.

The Business Case for Employee Participation

More and more, employers and benefits managers find themselves asking, "What can be done to improve my employees' understanding of health care coverage costs?" Getting employees involved in the process of coverage decision-making is a great way to improve their understanding of the costs, and in some cases may help keep costs down. But that's not the only way employee participation makes good business sense:

- Employee participation will ensure that employees have accurate information about costs (theirs and yours). Without active involvement, employees may not know how much you are paying and for what. They may simply assume that their premium covers the cost of their health insurance and fail to appreciate the company's contribution. Participation can limit their complaints about the exclusions and limits of any plan (see exhibit 5-3). This will limit your time spent addressing these complaints.

- Employee participation can also limit the costs of health coverage. Because employees who participate in planning will understand that they share the costs of health coverage, they will be motivated to eliminate unnecessary services and explore other ways to restrain costs.

- In a related vein, active employee participation will help employees understand what they can realistically expect from their health benefits. Without participating, they may honestly believe they can buy a Ferrari for the price of a Toyota. (Now, to be clear, we think Toyotas are very good cars—we both own Toyotas and have been very pleased with them—but still, Toyotas are not Ferraris.) Active participation will lead to more reasonable expectations about what types of insurance can be had for their (and your) money. This should, in turn, lead to more realistic employee demands of their health care coverage. Recall the study we mentioned in chapter 4, about how employees who understood their health plan and how it was picked were more satisfied than those who didn't, even when their

EXHIBIT 5-3
DECIPHERING THE
ALPHABET SOUP

One of the keys to effective employee participation is making sure they understand the terminology. Just when an employee starts to get clear about the difference between an HMO and a PPO, the FSAs (HCFSAs and DCFSAs) come in alongside the CDHC, the HRA, the HDHP, and the HSA. One simple way to make the most of employee participation is to give them resources and opportunities to learn about these new wrinkles in the system. In chapter 3, we provided a glossary of terms used in this book, including those listed above. The Ethical Force Program has also produced a brochure that you can hand out to your employees that explains how health care coverage decisions are usually made, and how to get help when they need it (you can order copies of the brochure at www.EthicalForce.org).

By the way, here are the acronyms above, spelled out:

HMO: Health Maintenance Organization

PPO: Preferred Provider Organization

FSA/HCFSA/DCFSA: Flexible Spending Account (Health Care FSA, Dependent Care FSA)

CDHC: Consumer-Driven Health Care

HRA: Health Reimbursement Account

HDHP: High-Deductible Health Plan

HSA: Health Saving Account

plan was not as rich? The same holds true here. Better understanding, even of a frustrating situation, creates more satisfaction.

• Employee participation in health care coverage decisions can also increase your retention rate. In some cases, employees will change jobs to get the health benefits that they or their family members need, or even just to have more and better choices of benefits. Many employees will not complain to you first; they will simply start looking around. But when employees participate in coverage planning, this gives you better and more timely information about their satisfaction or dissatisfaction. You then stand a better chance of creating benefits packages that address employee needs, which can keep them from leaving in search of better benefits.

Offering Employees the Opportunity to Participate

The best health coverage decisions depend on the proactive pursuit of employee participation, not just sitting back and waiting for employee input to come to you. This pursuit of information can take a number of forms. Here are some recommendations to help you solicit employee participation efficiently.

Committees

Invite employees to be committee members. By making employees or their representatives members of committees that work on benefits decisions, you signal the high priority assigned to employee participation. A seat at the table has both symbolic and actual value. Identifying specific representatives also indicates the expected contact person for employee concerns, clearly identifying the stream of communication.

What your employees need and want regarding health benefits will probably change over time. Having a committee with employee representatives can streamline the means of employee input and help keep benefits decisions in line with changing life circumstances of existing and new employees, not to mention the changing landscape of benefits themselves.

Record and distribute committee meeting minutes. If you have a committee to consider health benefits, then there should be written minutes of committee meetings to summarize their deliberations. The minutes, or some form of a summary, can be very valuable to convey the actual impact of employee participation on decision-making. The minutes are most valuable when they are distributed to employees as a record of the concerns raised and issues discussed during these meetings. The minutes also produce a paper trail that indicates the issues under consideration and the rationales for decisions that were made. In the event that some decision is challenged, these minutes may prove especially useful in reconstructing and explaining how the decision was made, and perhaps why not every concern could be accommodated.

Proactive Outreach Activities

Alongside the committee work suggested above, outreach activities are an important step to foster participation from employees who are not serving on committees. While employee committee members are in a good position to provide meaningful participation, only proactive outreach activities can ensure that their participation is representative of other employees' concerns. These outreach activities can vary in their complexity and the effort required.

Meeting announcements, input forms, and open forums. Some relatively easy but important activities are to announce scheduled committee meetings, post contact information for the employee members of the committee(s), provide a feedback box for human resources issues, and hold open forums for employee questions. Using these ideas to foster employee input before decisions are made puts employees' concerns in a position to actually affect the decisions and, equally important, shows employees that their concerns matter. Similarly, scheduling open forums on health care benefits (perhaps along with other human resources issues) also gives employees an opportunity to vent some of their frustration and will allow you to clarify any misconceptions or misunderstandings they may have about their coverage or how it is selected.

Educational activities. For organizations facing more difficult coverage decisions, there are a number of very engaging means to spark and distill employee participation about health care coverage. Drs. Susan Dorr Goold and Marion Danis have created the CHAT (Choosing Healthplans All Together) Program (see case 2 in "Case Studies" below). This has proven useful in a number of contexts by giving stakeholders an opportunity to be involved in making coverage decisions as well as fostering an understanding of the difficulty of making these decisions.

Surveys. For some companies it can be very helpful to solicit employee input through formal telephone, mail, or email surveys and focus groups. Sampling employee views via survey provides a reliable information base, if enough people respond to the survey. Equally as important, doing a survey creates a formal record of employee interests that can be used in making future coverage decisions and explaining to employees why decisions were made as they were, and it can then be followed up with future surveys to assess improvement or discover new or changing problems.

Why Wouldn't an Employer Be Participatory?

Of the Five Ethical Guideposts, this one has been the most difficult to nail down for many business decision-makers. In our conversations with human resources professionals and business leaders, we have heard over and over that employers would like to foster employee participation in health coverage decisions, but they have doubts that it will work out well—and fears that it could work very poorly. Here's why, and here's what we've heard in response to these concerns by employers who have taken steps to involve their employees in the process.

"Employees Don't Know What They Really Want."

Sometimes employees' ideas about their health coverage are superficial or based on misunderstandings, or just plain ignorance, of the complexities of the health insurance market and health care systems. It is the rare employee who is an expert on health insurance issues, and that employee is usually in human resources to begin with.

Well, as tempting as it might be to work only with "experts," other employees can still offer a great deal of valuable input. Employees are familiar with their own experiences and needs, and they can report past problems. Even though they might not always know exactly what they want, or what is available or realistic, employees *are* familiar with their circumstances in a way no one else can be. More importantly, once a program is in place to foster employee participation, some employees do become experts. And they can then serve as a homegrown, trusted resource for your other employees.

"Employees Won't Take No for an Answer."

By asking employees to participate, some employers fear that they are opening Pandora's box. Once employees are asked to provide input, they will expect it to be put directly into practice. If they request coverage for a particular service, they should automatically get it. To some readers this might seem exaggerated, but it is a very real concern for many others. For example, we were told point blank by one employer that he had no intention of asking his employees what they thought about their health care coverage, because he couldn't afford to change anything and he didn't want to raise their expectations.

More typically, though, when a system is put in place to solicit employee input, relatively few employees become directly involved.

And those who do become involved might be the ones who are most dissatisfied. That's why it's also important to have proactive means of collecting information from a greater number of employees. It also points to the importance of being prepared to make clear why particular requests or suggestions were not put into practice. If some employees asked for something that was not financially feasible, say so. If a choice had to be made between two options with supporters on both sides, make it clear that both options had supporters and explain what tipped the balance. Avoiding the appearance of secretive decisions can help employees deal with disappointment. Finally, if this seems to be a real problem for your organization, it might be helpful to ask employees directly about their level of participation in the process after the fact. Talking with employees, one on one or in groups, about why they were or weren't satisfied with their participation in the process can help identify what specifically led to out-of-control expectations for benefits.

"No Matter What Decisions Are Made, Some Groups Will Be Left Out."

Barring the creation of a health plan that offers everything and costs nothing, someone is going to be disappointed that what they want isn't covered, or the price is too high. In particular, people with unusual medical needs, regardless of their enthusiastic participation, are especially likely to feel that their needs haven't been taken into account in the final health care coverage decisions. In some cases, completely justifiable limits on cost and value will limit what is covered. In other cases, though, the exclusion of some services may result from decisions that have actually been skewed or biased during the process of decision-making. Either way, it is important to find out about this. In fact, the potential for less-than-ideal or unfair health coverage decisions does not suggest that employers abandon all efforts to solicit meaningful participation. Rather, it requires vigilance to ensure that these solicitations are purposefully directed to procure input from *all* stakeholders.

Case Studies

The two cases in this chapter illustrate success stories in meeting the challenge of soliciting employee participation. Some steps described might not be feasible or applicable for some companies. Don't despair—adequate participation is possible with any set of employees and with limited funds.

Case 1: Using an Employee Advisory Committee Effectively

In 2002, Ed Fox, the executive director of the Northwest Portland Area Indian Health Board (NPAIHB),[1] felt it was time to address the issue of domestic partnership in the health advocacy organization's benefits policies. The NPAIHB had extended the 100 percent employer-paid premium for health and dental coverage from employees to spouses and dependents a few years prior, but not to domestic partners.

Though domestic partnership often refers to same-sex relationships, many families, including heterosexual couples, choose to maintain domestic partnerships instead of legal marriages. As an organization that operates in accordance with Indian values, including close, immediate, and extended family ties, the NPAIHB had a particular interest in the issue.

To craft a policy, Ed requested employee volunteers for a committee that would examine the policies of employers currently covering domestic partners. The committee included employees who would directly benefit from domestic partner coverage, employees who were simply interested in the issue, and employees from finance and management who could bring their practical business expertise to bear on the issue.

The committee considered many existing domestic partner coverage policies and weighed a range of challenging issues. Would domestic partners' dependents be covered? Had organizations that offered coverage discovered any unintended consequences? (For example, increased employee tax liability was one such consequence the committee discovered. Because domestic partner coverage is considered by the IRS as income to the family, it increases the tax burden of those choosing to cover domestic partners and their dependents.)

Finally, the committee crafted a policy they felt was appropriate for NPAIHB and presented it to the organization's attorneys for review. The next step was to present the plan to the personnel committee. This is a standing committee of NPAIHB chair-appointed delegates who review personnel issues and propose policy changes. The delegates are identified via tribal resolution from the forty-three federally recognized tribes in Washington, Oregon, and Idaho.

The personnel committee recommended approval for the plan adding domestic partners to the list of parties eligible for coverage under NPAIHB's health and dental plans. Despite the fact that this would result in additional expenses to NPAIHB, the support by the overall delegation was immediate. One delegate said it was, "the only ethical thing to do."

It is fair to say that NPAIHB did a very effective job of getting employee input into this complex and controversial benefits design decision.

By requesting employee volunteers for the needed committee work, the NPAIHB got employees involved right from the start of the decision-making process. Every employee, whether or not they worked on the committee, participated in the process by deciding how to respond to this request. Calling for volunteers tells employees that their participation is welcome.

In addition, Ed went out of his way to get both obvious and not-so-obvious stakeholders on the committee. In this way, NPAIHB signified the need for participation from all stakeholders. Of course employees who will be directly affected by the benefits under consideration should be included—and they are more likely to volunteer. But for most decisions, all employees can be affected, either directly or indirectly, and so a broad range of employees should be included in the process. In the case of NPAIHB, employees with domestic partners have the most at stake. Failing to include their input could make the whole process a waste of time by producing a benefit that is unhelpful or that they don't want. But employees without domestic partners also need to be involved—if for no other reason than that they can carry back to their colleagues the fair and inclusive process that took place in making the decision.

There are other reasons to have a balance of directly affected and indirectly affected employees on the committee. "Balance" is the key word here. Including employees from across the organization can provide balanced input. These other employees can inform the committee about general perceptions of the change, general support (or not) for the benefit offering, or even if the change is likely to spark feelings of unfairness or demands for other changes. This balance can only be achieved by including employees who are indirectly affected, if at all, by the benefits being considered.

Finally, employee interests are not the only interests to be considered when making coverage decisions. The institutional review process of NPAIHB (through the personnel committee) ensured that employee interests were also balanced with other stakeholder interests, including the long-term broader interests of NPAIHB as an organization.

In this case, we have been quite narrowly focused on employee participation in benefits design. In some cases, employees should participate in administrative (or case-specific) decisions as well. If your company self-insures, for example, then some part of the appeals process might be done in-house. This raises a number of legal issues, primarily related to privacy and the separation of your business functions (such as hiring and firing) and your company's self-insurance functions, which we cannot cover here. But if you are responsible for some part of the appeals process, then, like the benefits design, the process should include employee participation. At minimum, employees should be involved in establishing the general criteria and processes for how appeals will take place.

Case 2: Reaching Out for Employee Input

The CHAT (Choosing Healthplans All Together) program, developed by bioethicists at the National Institutes of Health (NIH) and the University of Michigan, provides an opportunity for enrollees to become acquainted with the trade-offs that are a necessary part of health coverage decision-making. The CHAT program is not designed to produce a fully defined benefits package, but it is a very useful and engaging educational tool.

The CHAT program is essentially a board game (a computerized version is also available) that asks small groups of employees to develop a make-believe health plan given the constraints of a fixed budget. They have to come to agreement on how to ration the benefits available within the budget, represented by placing a limited number of pegs into holes on the game board. The game board includes holes for typical categories of health coverage, such as vaccinations, emergency care, and catastrophic care. After making their choices together, each player is dealt a hand of cards that gives him make-believe Health Events—and gets to see how well the health plan the group designed together would (or would not) cover the expenses associated with this event.

Schweikart Corp., a large family-owned manufacturer in the Seattle, Washington, area, used CHAT when the company's owner could see that the company was about to face a big premium increase, some of which was going to have to be passed along to employees. Even though this would be the first major increase in workers' monthly health insurance contribution in eight years, the owner was worried that employees might be very upset if they didn't understand why it was happening.

As the first few groups were brought together to play the game, they were surprised by the difficult trade-offs that were necessary to design a good health plan. Many said they had had no idea that health insurance was so expensive. It was obvious that they were developing a deeper understanding of the need to pay more if they wanted to maintain the good coverage they had all come to expect.

One unexpected result from using this educational tool is that some of the small groups got together after the game and wrote memos to Schweikart's human resources department leaders, offering constructive feedback on how they would be willing to eliminate certain existing benefits from the health plan to save money for themselves and for the company.

Schweikart Corp. is in a position where many companies, large and small, find themselves: the costs of continuing to provide employees with the same health care coverage have become unsustainable. At the same time, a sudden increase in employee costs for health coverage can have a negative effect on employee satisfaction, retention, and even productivity.

The management of Schweikart Corp. could have simply announced their decision and tried to limit the negative effects through an internal public relations campaign. Instead, by opting to use the CHAT program, they educated their employees about the difficulties of health coverage decision-making, and prepared them to participate effectively in the decisions that affect them.

One feature of the CHAT program that Schweikart did not use, but that is available, is the option to structure the CHAT games around the exact budget and the benefits available and under consideration by the company. Under this option, while playing the game, employees are also participating directly in helping to make actual decisions about coverage options.

As companies change and grow over time, the CHAT program and similar educational materials can be used to introduce employees to the difficulties of making these decisions for the company, while also preparing them to make personal decisions about the offered benefits packages. At the start, some young, unmarried employees might tend to choose high-deductible plans, while the advantages of an HMO might be clearer to the breadwinner of a family of four. But after playing the game and "experiencing" the effects of certain health events, some of these choices might evolve, and at least they will be better informed. The CHAT program can also introduce employees to new types of benefits packages in a way that helps them understand the advantages and limitations of these packages.

The value of interactive educational materials like the CHAT program lies in their ability to tangibly illustrate the obstacles and trade-offs involved in good decision-making about health care coverage. Educated employees will not only make better decisions for themselves, but provide better and more useful feedback for the final decision-makers in their company.

Conclusion

This chapter has offered specific steps to follow the Ethical Guidepost of making your decision-making process *Participatory*. The foundation of this Ethical Guidepost is that employee participation can help employers make better decisions about health care coverage. In the short term, employee participation provides input that is otherwise unavailable and that improves the quality of decisions made. In the long term, it gives employees a sense of understanding and ownership of the decisions that are made and plans that are chosen, which in turn lends quality, credibility, and legitimacy to these benefits coverage decisions.

Note

1. This is the single case in the book where actual names are used, with permission of the NPAIHB.

You Can Count On It

The Decision-Making Process Should Be *Consistent*

R *unRight Auto Parts Corp. is considering a new and contro-versial step to handle skyrocketing health costs. Starting at their next open enrollment, they will be charging employees who smoke $50 more per month for their health insurance premiums.*

Some of RunRight's benefit managers are very skeptical. In addition to the threat of bad publicity, they're worried that the company could lose some good workers who don't want to pay higher premiums or who object to the policy on principle. Future recruitment could suffer too.

One human resources executive pointed out that the policy isn't likely to stabilize company health costs. She noted that health risks associated with smoking don't seriously affect smokers until later in life, and RunRight's employees are mostly in their twenties and thirties.

Despite these objections, RunRight's human resources depart-ment notified employees about the targeted premium hikes a few months before open enrollment. Some have complained that the plan is discriminatory because certain workers might have a ge-netic predisposition for nicotine addiction. Why should they pay more for their premiums than someone who was genetically pre-disposed to, say, high blood pressure? Others have complained that it's inconsistent to target smokers as the only ones making risky "lifestyle choices." Couldn't a worker who drinks a lot or is obese, or who goes mountain climbing on the weekends, incur health care costs that are even greater than one who pays higher premiums because he or she smokes?

What do you think of RunRight's new policy? Is it fair to charge higher premiums to employees who smoke, given that they are statistically more likely to incur major health costs for the firm over the long haul? Or, looking at it the other way, is it fair to offer the same premiums to all employees, when some of them are doing things (like smoking) that are likely to drive up their health costs, while others are actively trying to curb those costs by making healthy lifestyle choices?

The employees challenging the new policy at RunRight are questioning whether the new premiums are equitable to all employees. In plain language, they don't think it is fair to treat one group of people differently than another, just because one group happens to choose to smoke. Those who are in favor of the change, however, believe the differences between those who smoke and those who don't are big enough that they warrant treating them differently—by charging them more for their health insurance.

The Ethical Guidepost at issue here is *Consistency.* In health care coverage decisions, being consistent means making the same decisions under the same circumstances. Are people in similar situations being treated similarly? As we mentioned in chapter 2, in philosophy the word for this type of fairness is "equity." Of course, philosophers aren't talking about equity as the term is used for margin trading, or about the equity you might hold in your house. They're talking about equity in the dictionary sense of a decision being "just, impartial, or fair." But just like in the stock market, equity with this definition has real value when you are making health care coverage decisions.

In this chapter, we'll look at four key ways for employers to improving the consistency, or equity, of their health care coverage decision-making processes.

Ethical Guidepost #3

Consistency: Your processes for designing and administering health benefits should result in similar decisions under similar circumstances.

Four Steps to Make **Consistent** Decisions

#1: Write out the values that guide your decisions about health care coverage and the way your company sets its coverage priorities—then follow them consistently.

#2: Look at the health benefits offered by competing employers in your community and try to at least provide benefits consistent with your competitors (if not better).

#3: Offer the same health benefits and options to all employees, regardless of their race, gender, sexual orientation, or other factors irrelevant to their health care coverage.

#4: Design benefits so that similarly serious types of health care needs are treated similarly, while important differences are taken into account.

Our gut sense of fairness is, in many ways, encompassed in the notion of equity, or consistency. So much so that the dictionary definition of equity, as we alluded to before, includes the term "fair." Even as very young children, the importance of consistency in decision-making made sense to us. The playmates of a child who cuts in line for the swings instead of waiting her turn shout: "That's not fair!" She interrupted the equitable distribution of turns on the swings. A teacher who says he will give *all* latecomers detention but enforces or ignores his rule depending on his mood, or, worse, because he likes some students better than others, quickly gets a reputation as unfair because of his inconsistency.

Because of this innate sense that fairness is related to consistency, an employer that makes obviously inconsistent health coverage decisions is very likely to run into trouble. At worst, inconsistent coverage decisions will be perceived as discriminatory and could lead to legal issues. But even far short of a lawsuit, an employer that is perceived as offering health benefits that are inconsistent is liable to have problems with employees. When confronted with unfair decision-making, individual employees' reactions vary. Some complain, but many don't—they just start looking for another job. In other cases, they might just stew and become more frustrated and less productive. On the other hand, having a process in place to foster consistent coverage decisions will help you fulfill your ethical obligations to your employees, while reaping the business benefits of a loyal workforce.

Finally, a key point of this chapter is that consistency in health coverage decision-making can be considered in at least two ways. First, health benefits can be consistent or inconsistent across employers in a similar industry. Second, benefits can be delivered consistently or inconsistently to the employees of one employer. Most businesses are well aware of the latter sense of consistency, while the former is considered less often. But both are important and will be addressed in this chapter.

Why Wouldn't an Employer Be Consistent?

In general, consistency is something that most employers strive for. In our interviews and focus groups, we did not hear anyone defend inconsistent decisions. And we heard a number of very strong defenses of strict consistency in decision-making, on the basis of legal liability for discrimination. But not all employers realize that full consistency is more than just not being blatantly discriminatory.

Full consistency entails looking at the health benefits offered by comparable employers, as well as ensuring that racial, gender, or more subtle forms of discrimination are not occurring within your workplace. Also, not all employers are aware of the importance of writing down coverage decisions and why they were arrived at, even though this is the only way to ensure that similar decisions are made from year to year.

Discrimination Isn't the Only Way to Be Inconsistent

Suppose that your company only offered health care coverage to male employees, or only to Latino employees. You would distribute the company's health care dollars inequitably and would undermine (if not eliminate) any semblance of fairness in your health care program! It's clearly unethical to privilege one subset of your employees over others based on factors (like race or gender) that are irrelevant to the decision to offer coverage. It might also be illegal. Plenty of related problems of inequities between employees within the workplace still arise (see case 3 at the end of this chapter for an example), but every employer we have spoken with understands the need to avoid basic race and gender discrimination.

But some employers offer health benefits that they know are far inferior to those offered at competing employers nearby. Doing this is not illegal. But it does lead to inconsistencies in health care coverage and could be perceived as unfair by the employees. Specifically, it is likely to lead one set of employees to sense that they are being treated unfairly compared to other employees in similar situations. This sort of cross-employer inconsistency is not completely avoidable—since no two employers are likely to offer exactly the same health coverage. And in some cases, inferior health benefits might be offset by better benefits in other areas, or better compensation generally. But it would be unfair to knowingly offer worse health care coverage than your competitors, and it would be especially unfair if the employees didn't know they were making this trade-off (see chapter 4, on the Ethical Guidepost of *Trans-*

parency). Several employers have also told us that misleading employees like this would be not only unethical but also unwise since, over time, this fact will become widely known. The harm to your reputation as a business, which might result from such a scandal, could prove hard to repair.

Inconsistent Bases for Decision-Making

Most employers can say what health care coverage has been offered each year for the past number of years. But not all can say why. As a result, each year a different set of values and priorities might drive the decision-making process. Of course, some priorities are constant, such as not breaking the bank on health insurance costs. But others might change over time (see exhibit 6-1). This is especially true if your coverage decisions are informed by employee input (see chapter 5, on the Ethical Guidepost, *Participatory*). Without a written set of health coverage priorities, employers are forced to make each year's health care coverage de-

---

EXHIBIT 6-1
CONSISTENT DECISION-MAKING
IN THE FACE OF CHANGING
CIRCUMSTANCES

As a company evolves over time, many factors may change with respect to its health benefits, including the size and characteristics of its covered population and the resources it has available for health care coverage. *Maintaining consistency over time is important—but that means consistent application of priorities, not maintaining identical benefits from year to year.* In the right circumstances, it can be ethical and consistent to limit coverage in leaner years, or to alter coverage when employees' needs change.

cision—and each decision along the way, if that is applicable—as if starting from scratch with no prior history. In fact, all employer decisions should be judged in the context of past and future health benefits choices. If you want to make coverage decisions consistently, you need to maintain a written explanation of the priorities on which you base all of your health benefits decisions. By maintaining your company's coverage priorities in writing, you can hold all the facts and choices you're faced with to a single standard, and apply this standard uniformly. You'll be able to justify your decisions—to yourself and to your employees.

What's the Business Case for Consistent Decision-Making?

Regardless of the amount of resources you devote to employee health, you as an employer can shore up your company's bottom line by making sure your decisions are consistent. Fair coverage practices help keep employees satisfied and productive, and they contribute to a healthy workplace.

- Employees who believe health care coverage decisions that affect them are being made inequitably or inconsistently will be disgruntled with your company. Retaining and recruiting top-quality employees is tough if current and prospective employees believe that they can receive more, better, or more consistent health care coverage from your competitors.

- Employees' productivity can decrease if workers lose trust in you and your company because they think you are making inequitable and inconsistent coverage decisions. In many workplaces, overall productivity depends on how well employees collaborate and work together in teams. Employees who feel that they are being treated unfairly, or who feel that their co-workers are unfairly receiving superior benefits, are unlikely to work well with each other. People who think others around them are getting a better shake create an atmosphere of resentment or distrust, which can destroy teamwork.

• No employee wants to get the news that his employer's contribution to his health insurance premiums is decreasing, or that his deductibles are about to increase. But if you have earned your employees' trust by making decisions in an equitable and consistent manner, they are less likely to look for other jobs, or to work at half-speed, if a financial squeeze forces you to limit coverage.

• In the worst-case scenario, employees who feel decisions have been made in a discriminatory way may sue your company. Expensive legal challenges distract your attention and your financial resources from your company's goals. Some misunderstandings might be inevitable, but they are more likely to turn into legal action if employees see a general pattern of inequitable and inconsistent decision-making.

Case Studies

The four cases in this chapter illustrate how several businesses have handled the challenge of making consistent health care coverage decisions. One warning before we begin: Some of the steps taken by these companies did increase the companies' up-front health care costs. We know that some businesses, perhaps especially smaller ones, cannot absorb even limited increases in health coverage costs. Techniques that involve cost hikes might not seem practical for these companies. Even if this is the case, don't despair. It is possible to distribute coverage dollars equitably and consistently whether or not your company has a lot of dollars to distribute. When pursuing fairness in health care coverage decision-making for your company, the size of the pie can be much less significant than how it's sliced.

Case 1: Establish Coverage Priorities in Writing

Saferide Auto Insurance had put a great deal of effort into designing its health benefits. The human resources department ran focus groups with employees to identify their top health care financing concerns. They summarized the company's coverage priorities and values on a Web site and in a booklet available in the human resources office.

As a modest-size company, Saferide's health coverage resources were limited and each year they had trouble getting reasonably priced premium offers from health insurers. In order to keep coverage affordable for all employees, Saferide's owners knew they needed to limit the benefits covered. Employees overwhelmingly expressed a preference for lower premiums that primarily focused on coverage for health conditions that threatened life or basic functioning.

Recently, Saferide employee George Young ran up against a coverage limitation and made an appointment to talk with his benefits manager. George had discovered, to his dismay, that only four doses of medication for erectile dysfunction were covered per month by Saferide's comprehensive health insurance plan.

When George lodged his complaint, his benefits manager handed him the benefits-priorities booklet that Saferide's employees and managers had crafted. George read it that night, but he wasn't convinced that his condition was being covered appropriately in light of the coverage priorities articulated in the booklet. He made another appointment with his benefits manager.

At their second meeting, George's benefits manager went over some of the steps that Saferide had taken in crafting their policies (George had been hired after the focus groups were held). Using data supplied by Saferide's insurer, the manager demonstrated how expensive coverage was just for life-threatening conditions and basic preventive care. George noted that for higher premiums, the company could get more comprehensive coverage, for example, coverage that did not leave him with major out-of-pocket costs for his erectile dysfunction treatment. His manager pointed out that higher premiums might put Saferide's plan out of the financial reach of many employees, but he offered to put the question to the employees in the next round of focus groups.

By maintaining a written document that outlines the goals and priorities of the health coverage, Saferide fulfilled Step #1 for consistent decision-making: *Write out the values that guide your decisions about health care coverage and the way your company sets its coverage priorities—then follow them consistently.*

Because he had this in writing, George's benefits manager could talk to him about how and why Saferide came to the decision that affects his erectile dysfunction coverage. The manager could outline the reasoning behind the limitation George objects to. Most importantly, he could demonstrate in a very tangible way why Saferide thinks it is important to provide equitable and consistent health benefits to all employees and dependents, even when doing so means that there may not be coverage for all areas of each individual's concerns.

George may or may not immediately accept Saferide's health care priorities, and he may remain unconvinced by the benefits manager's attempt to educate him about resource distribution. No matter what George's next move is, however, it is now informed by the fact that Saferide made good faith efforts to be equitable and consistent in their coverage. Of course, it doesn't hurt that Saferide has also been transparent and participatory in making its coverage decisions too!

Case 2: Look Around

The Palma family owns a small restaurant chain called Fisherman's Wharf Restaurants. A few of their restaurants stand alone, but most are surrounded by competition in areas with many eating establishments. Last year, the Palmas traveled up and down the coast, visiting their restaurants and speaking to their managers and employees.

Many managers working in high competition locations spoke of difficulties recruiting and retaining top-quality employees. Staffing challenges had become a real problem at the most popular locations; wait times were rising for customers, and tempers were flaring in the understaffed kitchens.

Over the years the Palmas had developed policies to ensure that their company was attractive to responsible, productive workers. They offered generous health benefits and their compensation packages were competitive with those of similar restaurants. Each of the Palmas' managers contacted their former employees to find out what had motivated their decision to resign.

As each manager reported his or her findings to the Palmas, a trend emerged. Many employees who had resigned had done so for the same reason: Fisherman's Wharf didn't offer domestic partner benefits, while other restaurants near the faltering locations did. The Palmas were out of sync with the competition. Perhaps this difference could account for their recruitment difficulties as well.

Due to rapid changes in benefits offered in their industry, the Palmas fell short of Step #2: *Look at the health benefits offered by competing employers in your community and try to at least provide benefits consistent with your competitors (if not better).* Because the Palmas' company fell behind community norms, specifically by not offering health benefits to unmarried partners of employees, their employees began to leave and potential employees found more attractive offers elsewhere.

If you're considering offering domestic partner coverage, you might be concerned that gains in employee recruitment and retention will be offset by increased health care costs due to your expanding covered population. You should know that domestic partner benefits are actually likely to be less expensive than benefits for married couples, because domestic partners tend to be younger and have fewer children.[1] The costs associated with your increase in covered lives will be at least partially offset by the stability of your employee population thanks to improved retention. You might also save money on employee recruitment, screening, and training.

While extending benefits to domestic partners can improve the fairness of benefits offered by some employers, this case is only meant to give an example of the benefits of Step #2. Maybe your company cannot afford to offer coverage to anyone but your workers. A tight budget doesn't mean you're being unfair. However, if funds become available for you to extend benefits to employees' spouses and dependents, offer it equitably by including domestic partners.

Case 3: Consistent Benefits Across All Employees

ABC Lawncare's employees span the salary spectrum, from the executives at headquarters to the lawnmowers at clients' homes. Reviewing their health costs for the year, ABC's owners were struck by how few of the lower-salaried workers had been buying into the health plans the company offered. In fact, many seemed to have no health insurance at all. The employees' lack of insurance was taking a toll on ABC. Over the past few years there was a pattern of workers taking multiple sick days due to conditions that would have been resolved more quickly if they had been caught earlier. As a result, understaffed Lawncare teams had been sent to jobs, new employees were sometimes not trained by older, more experienced workers, and more than one client had complained that quality was down.

In other bad news, the health insurer ABC had been working with for years notified them that their premiums would be raised significantly, after a few years of minimal increases. This was not entirely unexpected, as the company was approaching its twentieth anniversary, and the higher-salaried workers, who had been around since the beginning, were starting to have much higher health care costs, both for themselves and for the spouses and children that hadn't been around when ABC first got off the ground.

Hoping to solve both problems with one strategy, ABC Lawncare's benefits consultant suggested they adopt a salary-based health care program. This might get more of their workers insured and slow the increase in their premiums. She pointed out that the premiums for the coverage ABC offered constituted 30 percent of the lowest salaries they paid and 5 percent of the highest. No wonder the lowest-paid employees did not purchase insurance! By indexing workers' premium contributions to their salaries, the company could encourage more of its workers to get insured.

ABC established a set of tiers such that the highest-paid employees would pay approximately 75 percent of the cost of their premiums, while the lowest-paid would contribute only 25 percent. There was grumbling among higher-paid employees, of course, but they had already expected an increase. And when they gave the salary-indexed premiums a trial run, 70 percent of previously uninsured workers purchased insurance.

Even better, as the benefits consultant had predicted, premium costs rose much more slowly over the next several years, since the lower-paid workers were overwhelmingly younger and healthier than those employees with higher salaries. By making health insurance more affordable to the lower-paid employees, ABC redistributed health care costs among more employees and spread the risk of claims over a larger and healthier group.

Both direct and indirect health care costs were causing trouble for ABC Lawncare. Premiums were rising as their covered population aged and expanded with dependents, but this was not offset by adding in premiums from their younger, healthier groups of employees. Their lower-salaried workers' absenteeism was an indirect health care cost resulting from those employees' inability to pay for coverage or for access to timely health care.

Adopting a salary-indexed health program improved ABC's financial position on both of these fronts (see exhibit 6-2). Lower-

E X H I B I T   6 - 2
THE DIMENSIONS OF EQUITY

ABC Lawncare's bottom line improvements were produced
by a coverage design decision that made their benefits program more equitable. But, you may ask, how can it be equitable for some people (higher-paid employees) to pay a
larger share of their health costs than others (lower-paid
employees)? Couldn't that be seen as inequitable? The answer to this paradox lies in understanding the different
senses in which individuals can be in similar or different
circumstances. In one very narrow sense, all employees of
the same employer are similar. But in some very important
ways, all employees at ABC Lawncare are not similar. And
equity isn't just about treating similar people similarly, it's
also about treating people differently when they are different in important ways. Even though all of ABC's workers
have a common employer, different employees' financial
situations are obviously very different—and ABC's management has realized that these differences are important
because they affect how often the different groups of employees purchase health insurance coverage. A newly hired
ABC gardener is in a very different economic situation than
the ABC CEO. Indexing health care premiums to salary improved the equity of the firm's health plan because it made
health coverage more consistently available to every employee—and it did so by acknowledging the significant differences between them and treating them differently
because of these differences.

paid workers could take advantage of affordable health care coverage, and thus were less frequently absent due to untreated illnesses. Thanks to their increased number of covered workers, and the relative youth and health of their covered population, ABC's insurance premiums stabilized.

ABC's decision to provide salary-indexed health care coverage represents one way to address Step #3: *Offer the same health benefits and options to all employees, regardless of their race, gender, sexual orientation, or other factors irrelevant to their health care coverage.* By tailoring the cost of the coverage to employees' income, ABC allowed lower-salaried employees to participate in the benefit—coverage was therefore distributed over the whole group of employees, rather than being offered exclusively, in practice if not intent, to the higher-salaried employees who could afford it.

Another Salary-Indexing Strategy. Many employers use financial incentives such as co-payments, coinsurance, and deductibles to reduce health costs by encouraging employees to use health services only when necessary, without discouraging them from seeking treatment in the early stages of illness. However, out-of-pocket costs don't have the same effect on all employees; for example, as one recent article put it, "a $10 co-payment is not the same deterrent to someone who makes $120,000 a year that it is to someone who makes $12,000."[2] Therefore, to make these financial incentives effective, some employers have indexed co-payments and other out-of-pocket costs to employee salaries, instead of, or in addition to, indexing premium contributions.

Without indexing, financial incentives might not have their intended effects. At the higher end of the salary scale, employees won't have a real financial incentive to make cost-effective decisions about their health care. At the lower end, employees may avoid seeking treatment in the early stages of illness, as the associated out-of-pocket costs are an overly powerful deterrent.

An Innovation in Health Care Financing. Salary-indexed health care programs are not yet widespread. According to Scott

Wayne, a senior consultant in the Chicago office of Mercer Human Resource Consulting LLC, the idea is "at the chatter stage, but it's getting louder."[3] If this is your first time encountering the idea, you may immediately think of some drawbacks to such plans:

- *Health care coverage is challenging enough for a business to design and administer; won't creating salary-indexed coverage create more confusion and paperwork?*

  Employers who have adopted salary-indexed coverage acknowledge that some kinks must be worked out in the beginning, as in any other change in coverage. However, most who have used it have found it was not particularly difficult to establish their programs.

- *What happens when employees are promoted to a salary with a higher premium percentage to pay?*

  To avoid year-round administrative upheaval, you can have employees whose salaries change wait until open enrollment to begin paying their newly calibrated premiums.

- *If my company adopts a salary-indexed health care program, won't we have trouble attracting and retaining the best employees to fill our higher-paid positions?*

  Employers who have adopted salary-indexed health care programs say that it hasn't affected executive recruitment and retention because health care costs are a relatively small part of an executive compensation package.[4]

Case 4: Consistent Coverage Across Diseases

Topnotch Technology Co. is a small software development firm with approximately 150 employees. When Congress enacted the Mental Health Parity Act (MHPA), Topnotch owner Stephanie Smith and her benefits managers worked with their health plan to equalize mental health benefit dollar caps with the ones that applied to employees' medical benefits.

But Stephanie was very concerned that health care costs would increase beyond the firm's means with the equalized caps. So she and her managers took steps to limit mental health benefits, using tools that their attorney said were legal under the MHPA. They designed cost-neutral changes to Topnotch's plans that effectively maintained the difference between physical and mental health coverage.

Topnotch's revised plans either limited the number of mental health–related inpatient days and outpatient visits or had high deductibles on mental health care to discourage service use. Smith and her managers awaited the following year's cost totals, hoping that they had avoided any significant cost increases.

The next year, when Topnotch's benefit managers met with health plan representatives, they initially encountered some promising numbers. Not only had they avoided mental health care cost increases, mental health service usage and costs had declined significantly among employees. It looked like their cost-saving strategies had been successful.

Further analysis revealed a less rosy picture, though. Employees who had historically used mental health services had used significantly more nonmental health (that is, medical) services and had taken a greater number of sick days, compared to employees who had not used mental health services. No matter how they crunched the numbers, Topnotch's benefits managers had to admit that their savings in mental health services had been more than offset by the combined impact of greater medical costs and fewer days worked by employees. Smith and her managers headed back to the drawing board.

Like Topnotch, 87 percent of employers attempted to make cost-neutral changes in coverage that would maintain a physical/ mental health coverage disparity while bringing them into technical compliance with the Mental Health Parity Act.[5] Had they made meaningful changes to achieve mental health parity in their coverage instead, such employers would have been working toward Step #4: *Design benefits so that similarly serious types of health care needs are treated similarly, while important differences are taken into account.*

Mental illnesses can be as serious and debilitating as any physical illness. It's inconsistent to limit coverage for treatment based on the difference between health conditions that affect the mind and those that afflict the body. Physical and mental illnesses can create equally serious types of needs, and thus, for the purpose of achieving fair health care coverage, they should be treated similarly (see exhibit 6-3).

As it turns out, designing health care coverage with attention to mental health parity can improve not only the fairness of your health coverage and the health of your employees, but also the prosperity of your company. A recent study suggests that cutting mental health care coverage leads to added challenges for some employees with mental health problems without producing savings for employers.[6]

The case of Topnotch Technology illustrates how providing insufficient coverage for mental health services can be a self-defeating

EXHIBIT 6-3
REGULATORY BACKGROUND

The Mental Health Parity Act of 1996 requires that annual and lifetime dollar caps for mental health benefits must be no lower than dollar limits for medical and surgical benefits offered by group health plans. Employers with fifty or fewer employees are exempt from the law. Also, the law does not require employers to offer mental health services as part of their benefits package—nor does it preclude having different co-payments and other limits on mental health benefits. For more information, visit www.cms.hhs.gov and search for "mental health parity."

cost-cutting strategy. You may pay fewer mental health service-related bills, but losses in productivity, increased sick days, and greater use of nonmental health services by mental health service users can consume your savings. On top of all this, you'll also find yourself moving away from the Ethical Guidepost of *Consistency* in your health care coverage decisions.

The best estimates are that, at most, "mental health parity requirements—on both the federal and state levels—have increased employers' total health care costs by no more than about 1 to 5 percent, with the low end being closer to the norm."[7] Therefore, when designing your mental health benefits, remember that even if resources are limited, parity between mental and physical health coverage is not a government regulation to be circumvented—it's an important step toward fairness in health care coverage decision-making. Plus, you stand to gain a more productive and healthy workforce, savings on nonmental health services, and a more equitable and consistent health care program.

Conclusion

This chapter has offered specific steps to follow the Ethical Guidepost of making your decision-making process *Consistent*. Making consistent health care coverage decisions can provide tangible benefits for your employees' health and your own bottom line. While your company's health care budget may be tight, cutting fairness from your decisions will not improve employees' well-being or your company's financial health.

Notes

1. D. Berta, "Experts: domestic-partner perks bolster staffs' retention," *Nation's Restaurant News*, 38(19): May 10, 2004.

2. R.E. McDermott and J. Ogden, "Five ways to improve your health benefits program," *HR Magazine*, 40: August 1995; 44–48.

3. M.E. Podmolik, "Earn more, pay more," *Crain's Chicago Business*, 27(8): 2004.

4. Ibid.

5. G. Gonzalez, "Parity advocates aim to close loopholes in mental health law; employers, insurers oppose bill," *Business Insurance*, Aug. 9, 2004.

6. R.A. Rosenheck, et al. "Effect of declining mental health service use on employees of a large corporation," *Health Affairs*, September/October 1999; 193–203.

7. J. Greenwald, "Mental health parity not as costly as feared," *Business Insurance*, July 31, 2000; 3.

The Value Equation

The Decision-Making Process Should Be *Sensitive to Value*

*R*exco is a large retailer (over 50,000 employees) that has just completed an anonymous survey regarding its health benefits package. Many of the results were expected: More than half of the employees thought their plan cost too much, while more than half also thought it didn't cover enough. Some employees complained about specific coverage denials and others about the difficulty they had finding an "in-plan" physician.

Much more surprising were the responses to the substance abuse section of the survey. Rexco has prided itself on its support for employees with substance abuse problems and has consistently resisted efforts to have the coverage for rehab removed from the benefits package. At present, their policy is to cover admission to a month-long rehabilitation clinic.

What they hadn't realized was that this month-long absence indicated to all colleagues and coworkers what was going on. This made some employees very reluctant to use the rehab benefit because it came with the stigma of being publicly known as a substance abuser.

The results of the survey indicated that a large number of em-

ployees would not agree to the rehab program offered by the Rexco plan, even if they thought they had a serious substance abuse problem. And, more troubling, some had already sought out other rehab options without notifying the company or health plan. For example, some of the employees who had not admitted their problem to the company had successfully gone through a shorter immersion-type rehab program (a long weekend in a rehab clinic) followed by intensive follow-up.

Rexco had considered covering this type of alternative rehab several years ago, but declined because they could find no good evidence of its effectiveness. Now, the benefits department is wondering if declining this coverage was a mistake. It seems like this decision has kept some employees from getting coverage for their treatment, and it might have kept others employees from getting treatment for serious problems.

Rexco has been doing a lot that is right. While many employers, particularly small-to-medium-sized businesses, do not offer coverage for substance abuse treatment, Rexco has chosen to offer this coverage to its employees. That's good. Rexco is offering competitive health benefits (see chapter 6, on the Ethical Guidepost, *Consistent*). They also are inviting employee participation to improve the design of their benefits, by conducting this survey. That's good too (see chapter 5, on the Ethical Guidepost, *Participatory*). But do you think it's fair, or smart, for Rexco to offer only one kind of substance abuse coverage, especially now that they know that it is keeping some people with substance abuse problems away from treatment? On the other hand, if there is little information on the effectiveness of the newer treatments, is it fair, or smart, for Rexco to spend money on them?

The questions surrounding Rexco's coverage of substance abuse rehabilitation illustrate some of the challenges in making decisions about health coverage that are *sensitive to value*. Figuring out how to get the most value from the money you and your employees spend on their health plans is not easy. Information about costs and medical studies of effectiveness can be complicated enough. But there's even more to being sensitive to value than just cost and effectiveness. In this chapter, we'll look at three specific ways for companies to be sensitive to value in their health coverage decisions.

Ethical Guidepost #4

Sensitive to Value: Decisions about coverage should take into account both the standards of medical care and the needs and priorities of your employees.

Three Ways to Be **Sensitive to Value** in Decisions

#1: Use information about quality and outcomes for health plans, health-related services, and medical technology when making coverage decisions.

#2: When a new service or technology is significantly better than an existing alternative that you already cover, the new service should be covered.

#3: Gather employee input to make sure that your health care resources are spent on services that are truly of value to them.

The interrelationships between the Five Ethical Guideposts should be getting more and more obvious. In this case, to fully understand the value of a service, you really need to understand the values, and the health-related priorities, of your employees.

In addition, this guidepost draws attention to the fact that health care is an evolving field, so health care coverage is in constant evolution. Being sensitive to value means basing your coverage decisions on the most up-to-date information you can find. If your research reveals more effective or more efficient treatments, coverage decisions remain fair only if they can adapt to these changes.

Judgments of Value

Being sensitive to value requires a definition of what we mean by "value." When comparing treatments for the same disease, this process might seem pretty straightforward—which of the treatments is most effective and least expensive. But there are actually multiple components to the value of any health care service. Clinical effectiveness just looks at how well the treatment addresses the health problem. Cost-effectiveness can look at the comparative costs and clinical effectiveness of various possible treatments for the same health problem. But the personal value of a service can be different according to each person's priorities, the individual side effects they might experience, and even, as the case above showed, how the treatment is received around the workplace and in society.

Health care coverage decisions, both in the general design of the package and in the case-specific administration of benefits, should be sensitive to value in all of these ways (see exhibit 7-1). Each area presents a different set of challenges to you as a decision-maker.

Clinical Effectiveness

In most cases, questions of clinical effectiveness, in isolation, seem fairly straightforward—or at least they should be for doctors and other researchers who specialize in answering these questions. Does the treatment in question treat the symptoms, derail the disease process, or improve health? If it does none of these things, as a general rule, the decision for you is not too hard: The treatment should not be covered. In making decisions about coverage, it doesn't make sense—and it would be unfair—to spend resources covering things that don't work.

Although this sounds easy, if you have ever been involved in any appeals or decisions about special cases, you know that questions of clinical effectiveness are not always easy. For example, in the case that started this chapter, there was not clear and convinc-

EXHIBIT 7-1
SHORT-TERM AND
LONG-TERM VALUE

Pitney Bowes (an international office technology and service company) has become known for innovations in value-based insurance purchasing for its employees in the United States. The innovations of this company's health plan are too numerous to list here (some features have evolved multiple times), but perhaps their most daring innovation has been to knowingly pay more in short-term cost in order to get expected long-term gains. For example, they have provided in-house medical clinics that make it easy for employees to take advantage of fully covered cardiovascular and cancer screenings, among other things. They have also paid for on-site fitness centers with exercise physiologists to counsel and guide employee fitness activities.

This is a difficult thing to do in a climate of employee turnover and the expectation of instant results. But over time, Pitney Bowes managers have learned that investing money in more expensive but more effective ways to treat health problems is a better value, because seemingly inexpensive stopgap measures or less effective services can lead to recurrent illness. Ultimately, the "cheaper" option often turns out to be more expensive.

ing evidence that these shorter rehabilitation regimens worked reliably. Does that mean they are not clinically effective? Not exactly. The absence of evidence that something works is not the same as having evidence that it does *not* work. (And to make matters more complex, other considerations of value might still make coverage worthwhile, as we'll get to in a moment.) Also, any doctor will tell you that a number of treatments have been accepted as effective by the medical community over the years, and are now standard care, even though they lack research evidence. In many of these cases, it would be clearly unethical to subject the treatment to research (would you sign up for a research project where you might get a placebo instead of antibiotics for your pneumonia?). Of course, covering these "standard of care" services is generally advisable despite the lack of published studies that specifically prove they work.

Cost-Effectiveness

Two types of cost-effectiveness are important in making health care coverage decisions—the cost-effectiveness of comparing different treatments for the same health problem and the cost-effectiveness of comparing treatments for different health problems. The first kind of cost-effectiveness we could call "within-disease value analysis." It is often done using a technique called Cost-Effectiveness Analysis (CEA) (see exhibit 7-2). CEA can be quite complicated, and, thankfully, it's not usually done by employers looking at health coverage issues. It really should be done by experts in health services research, and in particular, those who don't have a stake in the outcome. Because of the complex math involved, and many different assumptions that must be made, cost-effectiveness studies that compare two treatments for the same disease are not too hard to "rig" to give one answer or another. As a result, cost-effectiveness studies should be carried out by impartial experts.

Even with impartial experts doing it, however, CEA is rarely a completely objective evaluation (like clinical effectiveness should be). It is rare for a treatment to have a single effect, so CEA must include trade-offs, and different potential outcomes have to be assigned "weights" in the equations. For instance, how much should an increased risk of disability weigh compared to a longer lifespan? Perhaps a more specific example here might help. There are

EXHIBIT 7-2
THE BASICS OF COST-
EFFECTIVENESS ANALYSIS (CEA)

There is a basic formula for looking at the cost-effectiveness of one treatment strategy compared to another. Here is the formula for comparing a new treatment strategy with current practice.

$$\text{CE ratio} = \frac{\text{cost}_{\text{new strategy}} - \text{cost}_{\text{current practice}}}{\text{effect}_{\text{new strategy}} - \text{effect}_{\text{current practice}}}$$

In this formula, the CE ratio is the "price" of the change in outcome purchased by switching from current practice to the new strategy. If, for example, the new strategy helps patients with the medical condition to live, on average, one extra year, and if, on average, the new treatment costs $10,000 more than the current practice, then the CE ratio would be $10,000/life-year. This is a very simple example, but hopefully it gets the point across. For the employer or a health insurer, if the cost difference is small enough compared with the change in effect, then the new strategy is considered "cost-effective." If a strategy is dubbed "cost-effective," it generally implies that it is a good value for money and should be adopted and covered.

two main options to care for men with prostate cancer, surgery and radiation therapy. Surgery leads to impotence more often, but it also cures the cancer more often. How should you weigh those different possible outcomes to get a single cost-effectiveness number? As you can see, whether or not different trade-offs are "worth it" are not simply questions of fact; they also include value judgments. To put it in nonmedical terms, think about comparing a

Gala apple and a Red Delicious apple. Even though both are apples, knowing which one costs more is likely to be just one factor among several in deciding which holds more value to you.

The second type of analysis, comparing the value of covering treatments across different diseases, could be called "across-diseases value analysis." This type of value analysis was alluded to in chapter 6 on the Ethical Guidepost *Consistent*. It is a different type of value analysis, using techniques that are somewhat different from CEA, and if anything, it contains even more value judgments than does CEA. More importantly, you are far more likely to be involved in making direct decisions about this type of value comparison. Common examples include decisions about whether to cover treatment for substance abuse, experimental therapies, or vision care. That is, rather than helping to decide whether to cover one or another possible treatment for a disease, this comparison is used to help decide whether to spend resources on treatments for one disease versus on other diseases.

Just like in CEA, it is possible to create a mathematical comparison between costs and the various effects of different treatments across diseases. But you can imagine that comparing effectiveness is not easy. If analyzing value within a disease is like deciding between a red delicious apple and a gala apple, analyzing value across diseases is like deciding between a gala apple and a banana. Even if the price is exactly the same (and even though both are in the same general category: foods), they do very different things and produce very different outcomes. Analyzing value across diseases depends fundamentally on what you (and your employees) want.

Employee participation is pivotal for good health care coverage decisions that are sensitive to value. Across-disease comparisons might produce very different results if your employees are largely young and single versus if they are mostly married couples with young children. The first are less likely to want comprehensive coverage for vaccinations and some other services that the latter are very likely to value highly. So for questions about across-diseases comparisons, you and your employees will have to ask: Given the limited resources available, is this a treatment worth covering? Knowing the trade-offs involved, is this a service with high value *for us*?

Personal Value

Finally, the personal, or individual, value of a service can also play a role in some coverage decisions. For example, side effects refer to the (usually unattractive) effects of a treatment aside from its effect on the disease process or symptoms (for example, radiation therapy sometimes has the side effect of hair loss). Clearly, a medical treatment that usually works well, but has terrible side effects in some people, would not be of value for those who get the side effects. In cases like this, coverage might need to include options for those who cannot use the typical treatment. It has become quite common for health plans today to cover certain drugs only when the patient cannot tolerate a "first-line" drug, for example.

More than this, however, we should also think of nonmedical issues as possible side effects of a coverage decision. Rexco's employees were not taking advantage of its drug rehabilitation benefit because of the side effect that the month-long absence could lead to a stigma. When a coverage decision is made regarding a certain treatment, being sensitive to value means not only thinking about the clinical effectiveness and cost-effectiveness of the treatment hypothetically, but also whether or not employees will actually use the covered benefit. If they will not, the resources set aside for the purpose may be flushed down the drain.

Centers of Excellent Value

One possible source of variability in the value of a service is the organization providing the service. Identifying treatments that are clinically effective and cost effective can be tied to finding hospitals, physician groups, and academic centers that are excellent and efficient at what they do. For example, the Shouldice Hernia Center in Ontario, Canada, might be the best place in the world to have hernia repair surgery. The recurrence rate of hernias after treatment at Shouldice is less than 1 percent, while on average the recurrence rate is closer to 5 percent (and at some hospitals, it's even higher). They also have rapid turnover and low rates of complications. For some employers, using a center of excellence like this, even if it initially costs a bit more, might lead to higher-value health care. As a bonus, some centers of excellence—including Shouldice—actually charge less for their specialized services than most other facilities, in part because they are more efficient.

Of course, for most employers it will not be feasible to send employees to Ontario for hernia surgery. But many local centers of excellence exist. Coupling these centers of excellence with covered benefits can have long-term positive effects—both on employee health and on your business's bottom line.

Determination of What? By Whom?

It might seem like any discussion of "value" is just a veiled discussion of cost. But we hope to convince you that this just isn't true. When coverage decisions are fully sensitive to value, the cost of the treatment is a serious consideration, but only after consideration of the clinical effectiveness of the treatment. No matter how inexpensive it is, covering an ineffective treatment will never show sensitivity to value. The cost of treatments is also balanced with the personal value associated with the treatment, such as side effects. If side effects are such that employees won't take advantage of covered treatments, covering them becomes unimportant. Here are four specific examples where sensitivity to value is very significant—and lower cost is not always a primary marker of value.

- First, sensitivity to value marks a preference for the least expensive of two equally effective treatments. For example, if a name brand and a generic antibiotic have been shown to be equally effective, it is more sensitive to value to cover the generic instead of the name brand version. In this case, cost is the key marker of value, because all else is equal.

- Second, sensitivity to value can also include judgments about which kinds of treatments should be covered. If a decision must be made between providing coverage for treatment for a rare disease and a common disease, both with equivalent effectiveness at similar cost, treatment for the more common disease has more value. In this case, cost is not directly relevant, because it is equal for both treatments.

- Third, inexpensive and effective treatments often hold great value, but some treatments are more valuable when they are performed at centers of excellence. Many standard therapies are equally effective almost anywhere (any dermatologist can remove a sebaceous cyst). But for more complicated care, such as a carotid endarterectomy to prevent strokes, even though it might seem cheaper to have the procedure carried out nearby, the long-term value of having this procedure performed at a center of excellence can easily outstrip any initial savings. In this case, cost estimates can be misleading, because the initial cost estimates might not reflect the situation in the long term.

- Fourth, being sensitive to value also means covering services that employees value. The values of employees, as assessed through their active participation, must contribute to coverage decisions so that employers can cover services that their employees actually want. In this case, cost-effectiveness can take a backseat in the assessment of services that are highly valued by employees (more on this in a moment). To be more specific, employees need not weigh in on whether they think a particular treatment will have a good outcome. Unless you run a company of medical researchers, how would they know? However, you do need to find out what your employees believe about the balance of benefits and costs involved with their coverage. Being sensitive to value is intimately related to being attentive to and fostering employee participation.

Why Wouldn't an Employer Be Sensitive to Value?

In talking with employers, human resources professionals, and consultants, we heard of relatively few barriers to considering value in making health care coverage decisions. But some employers thought of value as simply cost. When we delved more deeply, we came up with a few reasons why being sensitive to value in their health benefits hasn't always been a top priority in some businesses. We have also heard good answers to each of these issues.

1. *The cost of figuring out what is more or less valuable is too high, or it's not my responsibility anyway (that's what the health plan is supposed to do).*

Although we can't deny that there are some costs to being sensitive to value, the long-term costs of insensitivity can be much higher. From paying for ineffective treatments to paying too much for effective treatments, decisions that are not sensitive to value expend resources without return. In addition, if side effects push employees to seek alternative treatments, they will miss additional work. And if valued benefits aren't provided, employees can be less productive and loyal, or they could seek employment elsewhere.

In terms of your responsibility versus that of the health plan, this will depend a good deal on your specific situation. If your company is self-insured, then you obviously have an increased responsibility to understand CEA and the details of plan-design decisions—after all, you *are* the plan, even if you subcontract out for administration. But even for smaller companies, understanding what your employees value is worth figuring out. And it feeds into each of the other Ethical Guideposts.

2. *Changes in coverage benefits to remove low-value services won't help employee morale and, in some cases, will actually upset employees.*

As we all know, there's no exact science to predicting how employees will respond to changes in their health coverage. Changes in coverage that reflect changes in medical knowledge will not always be greeted by employees with satisfaction. If employees (and their doctors) have faith in a treatment regimen, they may challenge a coverage change even if it seems like it is based purely on clinical effectiveness research. Bear in mind, however, that these challenges are not always a bad thing. In some cases, getting complaints about a coverage change will warrant looking at the issue again. Especially if medical practitioners are complaining as well, it might mean the information is not as clear as it seemed.

Case Studies

The two cases in this chapter include difficult situations that illustrate the challenges of designing and administering health care coverage that is sensitive to value. The first addresses how the value of a service can change according to employees' needs and priorities. The second illustrates some of the difficult decisions made by companies that self-insure. Regardless the size of your company, being sensitive to value is an important Ethical Guidepost in your coverage decisions.

Case 1: Pushing the Mental Limits

PPOF, a small manufacturer with expanding prospects in the northeastern United States, has recently come up against a wall regarding mental health coverage for its employees. Until now, they have been able to cover almost all mental health treatments,

*but rising costs for both mental health and health care in general
have forced them to make some tough decisions about their cover-
ages.*

*Dominick West, the benefits/human resources director, has no-
ticed a very large increase in claims made for mental health treatments (they've even outpaced the increase in claims for heart
disease treatments). Jerry Davis, the CEO of PPOF, asks if there
are any easy ways to stop the dramatic increases in health coverage
expenditures. Dominick immediately suggests curbing or even
dropping their mental health coverage.*

*"Of course, part of the reason we would save so much by
limiting or dropping this coverage is that it's so popular. We risk
upsetting our employees if we cut it," Dominick is quick to point
out.*

*"Well," Jerry responds, "we need to cut something. We can't
keep paying for these increases. What do you suggest?"*

Dominick West and PPOF are in a position that many companies find themselves in today. How do you treat employees well,
provide good health benefits, and also maintain sustainable health
coverage costs? In recent years, mental health treatments have
been the second fastest growing area of health care expenditures,
and the outcomes of mental health treatments can be hard to measure. It is natural for Dominick West to think of this as a good
place to cut costs.

Before suggesting cutting or dropping the benefits, though,
the first step for Dominick West should be to evaluate the value
of the health plan that administers their mental health benefits.
For example, the Health Plan Employer Data Information Set
(HEDIS®) provides evaluations of managed care companies (see:
www.ncqa.org/Info/QualityCompass/index.htm). HEDIS® allows
companies like PPOF to evaluate how well managed care companies address various health issues, including mental health. Given
their recent increase in expense in this area, it would be worthwhile to evaluate their current health plan's performance regard-

ing mental health. Perhaps there is an option that would allow PPOF to offer equivalent or even better mental health coverage by using a center of excellence, for example.

In the event the services are being delivered well and at a reasonable cost, however, it might still turn out that the best place for PPOF to cut costs is in mental health coverage; but the best decision regarding whether and how to cover mental health should be sensitive to the value of these services to employees. That means PPOF needs to get employee participation in the decision process. This may not be easy, since employees could be less likely to speak up in an open forum about their mental health issues. But other methods of participation, such as anonymous questionnaires, might help to determine the value of the service. The high volume of mental health coverage claims already suggests that any cuts could be contentious. Dominick will probably find it necessary to explain in some detail why current coverage levels are unsustainable. It is not simply that management is limiting mental health coverage; instead, employees need to see that reducing the rate of growth of their health benefits costs is a necessary change to maintain fiscal stability for PPOF. Employees should then be invited to suggest whether other benefits would be better alternatives to cut.

It's difficult to predict how employees will respond to the admission of fiscal difficulty in maintaining the health benefits. Realistically, a mixture of skepticism and resignation is likely. Regardless, the message should be clear—some benefits must be trimmed or eliminated in favor of others. The question employees can help answer through their participation is, "Is mental health the best alternative to cut?"

Tempting as it may be to oversimplify this process, Mr. West and Mr. Davis (as well as PPOF's employees) should recognize that the decision is not simply cover or don't cover, but could include levels of coverage as well. Would it be better to continue covering certain aspects of mental health while eliminating others? And PPOF's managers almost certainly will point out that if they simply eliminate all coverage, they risk PPOF's productivity—

employees who are now being treated effectively might not be able to afford continuing treatment, leading to an increase in uncontrolled mental illness. And an increase in uncontrolled mental illness would likely have a negative impact on more than just the company's productivity.

Case 2: Should This Idea Take Off?

Daniel Stewart, director of human resources for Doering Airlines, was recently approached by his immediate subordinate, Gale Siminowski. She presented a plan that Daniel is considering, but he's not sure how seriously he should take it. Given the size of the company (over 20,000 employees), they have self-insured for the last ten years. This has led them to encourage employees, through a number of creative strategies, to maintain healthy lifestyles and eliminate unnecessary use of medical services. Despite these efforts, there has been a recent dramatic increase in the number of prescriptions for cholesterol-lowering drugs that are being filled. The costs to Doering Airlines are quite high, not only for their portion of the prescription costs, but also for the more frequent diagnostic tests and physician visits that accompany being on some of these drugs.

Gale's plan has a single aim: limit the number of prescriptions for anticholesterol drugs. One way to do this would be to simply stop covering them in the next plan year. This would create quite an uproar among employees, and it was not seriously considered. Instead, Gale suggested that Doering Airlines offer its employees incentives to lower their cholesterol as much as possible without a prescription. The most common ways to do this are through lower-fat diets and regular exercise. Her plan has two parts. First, is to offer food service that includes more low-fat foods and provide an exercise room with fitness equipment on-site for employees to use before or after work or during their breaks. Second, and this is what Daniel is much less sure about, is to offer premium reductions on their health care coverage for employees who successfully manage their cholesterol without medication.

This plan raises the concern that employees who do not have high cholesterol will feel cheated—they don't have a corollary opportunity to lower their premiums. Gale recommended addressing this concern through an active information campaign explaining the costs to the company of anticholesterol prescriptions and treatment as well as expected costs of the later effects of employees with uncontrolled elevated cholesterol (increased chance of heart attack, stroke, and so on). The company would pledge to use some of the savings on all employees, and the fitness room would be open to all employees regardless of their cholesterol level.

If Daniel gives the green light, Gale will crunch the numbers to work out the details of the plan.

Would it be fair for Doering Airlines to offer a special incentive to their employees with high cholesterol? Is this the best use of their health care coverage resources?

One of the first things to consider is the clinical effectiveness of this plan. Unfortunately, it would get a mediocre score. Elevated cholesterol is not simply a lifestyle choice. Certainly, lifestyle plays a significant role in an individual's cholesterol levels—good diet and regular exercise can lower bad cholesterol and raise good cholesterol. However, cholesterol also has a hereditary component. A number of individuals will be unable to lower their cholesterol to acceptable levels through lifestyle changes alone. Accordingly, Gale's plan might not be as clinically effective as the existing plan. On the other hand, Gale's plan doesn't preclude the use of prescriptions; it simply encourages other means to control cholesterol.

In terms of fairness, though, the fact that high cholesterol is hereditary for some employees might pose a problem—individuals who are hereditarily unable to control their cholesterol through lifestyle changes would be unable to get the discounted premium.

The cost-effectiveness of this plan would also need to be evaluated. Without specific numbers, this is impossible to judge. Daniel probably should not reject Gale's recommendation simply because it is unknown if the plan will be a more efficient use of resources.

Instead, his green light for pursuing the plan, if it is to be sensitive to value, would have to include the condition that the plan will be abandoned if the costs don't add up.

The role of personal values is probably the most difficult area to evaluate in this situation. On the one hand, implementing this plan could lead to a large number of disgruntled workers—those who don't have high cholesterol or can't control it through lifestyle changes. On the other hand, it could produce a number of side benefits for all employees—such as the presence of the on-site gym and the healthier food in the cafeteria. The availability of fitness equipment would be a boon for all employees interested in convenient and regular exercise. This could also lead to decreased use of medical services and out-of-pocket costs for them as well. Further, some employees who do not currently have high cholesterol might get it in the future—then they would become eligible for the plan.

There are a number of variations or modifications to Gale's plan that, so long as they are cost-effective, might be considered too. First, the plan could offer premium discounts to *any* employee who attains a certain body-fat percentage, or some other marker that is associated with good health. This would include many of the employees with high cholesterol, but would also give other employees an incentive to improve their health, or to remain healthy. Second, the plan could be introduced as the first in a series of steps to encourage healthy living. Future steps might include incentives for employees to control high blood pressure or to make other lifestyle changes, such as to stop smoking.

One way to modify Gale's plan that would probably be seen as unfair would be to first increase the premium for employees with high cholesterol and then offer a reduction if they control their cholesterol through diet and exercise. Although the incentive would still be in place, this would essentially punish employees whose high cholesterol is hereditary, since they would be treated inconsistently with the rest of the employees. For further discussion of this issue, see chapter 6, on the Ethical Guidepost *Consistent*.

Conclusion

This chapter has offered specific steps to follow the Ethical Guide-post of making your decision-making process *Sensitive to Value*. Whether you cover a few employees or many thousands, it is worth your while to carefully consider the value of the health benefits you offer. Considering value doesn't just mean looking at the price tag, it also means understanding what works and what doesn't. Given the rapid pace of change in health care, this is more than a full-time job, and it's probably one you share with a health plan. But using resources like HEDIS® to evaluate the performance of health plans is an important first step that every employer can take. In addition, being fully sensitive to value means understanding what you and your employees want from your health care coverage. There's no point in covering benefits that your employees don't want or can't or won't use. At the same time, there's great gain to be had in crafting a benefits package that is sensitive to the needs and priorities of your employees.

Stay Flexible

The Decision-Making Process Should Be *Compassionate*

*I*n response to a number of employee requests, FitWell, a regional clothing retailer with about 200 employees, is looking
to change their health plan. Employees have been requesting a
shift to a health plan with lower premiums. After negotiating and
conversing with several national insurance companies, Anna
Mueller, FitWell's owner, found an HMO that met with general
employee support. Some employees expressed reservations about
the restrictions on in-network physicians, and one employee in
particular, Aaron Dufresne, expressed serious concern about this
restriction. Yet, Anna had carefully looked at the quality measures
available and overall this HMO was quite good. She decided to
change to the HMO. Her employees' concerns seemed to fade and
most employees seemed to have endorsed the change.

In the weeks after the decision to change plans, though, Aaron
approaches Anna and explains the reasons for his reservations. He
has recently been diagnosed as HIV+ and feels he needs to continue his relationship with his physician. The relationship goes
back twenty years, and he worries about the transition to a new
physician and whether he'll even get along with someone new.

Anna listens to his frustrations and after he has finished, expresses sympathy for his position, but, she explains, she had to focus on the best plan for her entire group of employees. She also expresses her concerns for Aaron's vulnerable position, but emphasizes that the decision has already been made.

Aaron explains, "If I can't go back to my doc through my insurance here, I'm going to have to look for another job where I can. You know I don't want to leave. I've been here so long, and I love these people and this company, but I really need to know I can trust my doctor. Isn't there anything you can do?"

Would it be fair for Anna to make some accommodation for Aaron, knowing that she couldn't do it for all her employees? Anna is in a difficult situation. During plan selection she was transparent, she solicited employee participation, she considered the quality of care the HMO could offer, and the plan appears to be consistent with the values and needs of most employees. And yet, here she is facing a difficult situation with Aaron Dufresne. On the one hand, she wants to help him get the best health care from his chosen physician. On the other hand, she can't govern the health plan according to every single individual employee's needs or wants.

It's certainly not unusual to want to continue a long-term patient-physician relationship. In the case of Aaron Dufresne, this desire is heightened by the timing of the possible disruption. Aaron's recent HIV+ diagnosis puts him in a particularly vulnerable position which, in the worst cases, could lead to depression with all of its problems and risks. Would it be compassionate for Anna to help Aaron maintain his existing relationship with his physician? It seems that it would be. But would it be fair (see exhibit 8-1)?

In this chapter we'll look at what it means to be compassionate in making health care coverage decisions. You may recognize the case above from chapter 1. We've used it again here because it highlights the role of compassion in fair decision-making. As we will discuss, the concept of compassion can be slippery—we may

EXHIBIT 8-1
SIMILAR, OR DIFFERENT?

Early in the book, we discussed a classic definition of fairness as equity—treating similar situations similarly and different situations differently. To decide if an exception is warranted for Aaron, we need to decide whether Aaron's case is different enough from other employees to warrant different treatment.

know compassion when we see it, but describing it can be quite difficult. What's more, there are some heart-wrenching cases where the Ethical Guideposts of *Compassion* and *Consistent* are in tension, if not in direct conflict. But compassion is a key feature of ethics in health care—after all, health insurance is fundamentally a way to spread costs to make sure we can take care of the most vulnerable among us at their time of greatest need. Each of us, at some time, might need to rely on compassion within the health care system. So if we want it to be there for us when we need it, compassion must be an Ethical Guidepost in making fair health care coverage decisions.

Ethical Guidepost #5

Compassion: Health care coverage decisions should be flexible enough to meet the needs of individuals with unique health problems.

Five Ways to Demonstrate **Compassion** in Decisions

#1: Evaluate the health effects of benefits design decisions (such as exclusions, waiting periods, service caps, and co-payments) on especially vulnerable people.

#2: Clearly address the priority given to services for your employees who have catastrophic medical needs.

#3: Provide a choice of supplemental benefits options that are tailored to employees with special needs.

#4: Track your employees' uptake and use of supplemental benefits options and use this information in future revisions to your basic benefits package.

#5: Monitor how other organizations respond to the needs of your employees, such as how your health coverage provider responds during an appeal.

Types of Compassion

Although the different types of compassion that can be expressed by humans might very well be innumerable, in this chapter we'll split compassion into two categories: systematic compassion and episodic compassion. Systematic compassion happens during benefits design, and it occurs at the institutional or structural level. Systematic compassion attempts to set the backdrop for health care coverage as flexible and able to respond to predictable particularities. Episodic compassion happens at the level of individual coverage decisions, and it addresses the occasional circumstance that can challenge even the best-designed health benefits package. Episodic compassion arises from extreme circumstances that call for at least the consideration of additional, unplanned coverage.

Systematic Compassion

Meeting every preference of every employee is simply not possible in designing health benefits, and making exceptions to the existing health coverage should be reserved for rare, exceptional cases. Nonetheless, accommodating employees' diverse preferences is almost always possible without having to make frequent exceptions. It just requires attention to systematic compassion. For example, one expression of systematic compassion is to provide a number of distinct (that is, meaningfully different) health plans for employees to choose among. Of course not every employer can do this. Smaller employers, in particular, generally don't offer more than one plan. But even then, systematic compassion can also be expressed through offering supplemental coverage to employees.

For Aaron Dufresne, for example, Anna might express systematic compassion if she were to offer multiple plans, at least one of which would allow him to keep his current doctor. Or, perhaps she could offer a way for him to continue seeing his doctor by purchasing supplemental coverage. These options would allow him to maintain his relationship with his physician without the risk of being seen as unfair to other employees.

Systematic compassion, however, is not just about providing alternative coverage options to employees. It's also about being attentive to how vulnerable groups and individuals will be affected by the health coverage. If vulnerable individuals or groups are not considered, compassionate decision-making is not possible. For example, even in small companies, there is a reasonable chance that an employee or family member will need catastrophic care in the course of a year. If the benefits design process ignores this significant possibility, it can't be fair. Because not only would it fail to address the real health care needs of employees, but it would fail to address their needs at the worst possible time—when employees and their families are the most vulnerable.

Which vulnerable people should be taken into consideration? That will depend on your particular situation, of course, but bear in mind that employees can be vulnerable for reasons independent of their health. Employees who lack savings, who are more susceptible to disease, who already require chronic care, or who are likely to have difficulty obtaining care from the health care system (such as foreign-language speakers or people with low literacy) are all vulnerable to unfairness in health care. What your business should do will depend on the size and make-up of its workforce, whether or not it is self-insured, and other factors. But in any event, failing to think specifically about the effects of your benefits design decisions on especially vulnerable employees would not be fair.

In the case of Aaron Dufresne, it is too late for systematic compassion. To Anna's dismay, the plan for the year is set, and so she is faced with the question: Should she respond to Aaron's request on an individual basis, and if so, how?

Episodic Compassion

After catastrophic events or because of other life circumstances, individuals can become particularly vulnerable in their need for health care services. Like national efforts at rescue and recovery after a calamity, episodic compassion is expressed through our response to these unusual situations. When parents find out that their son or daughter has cancer or when the disability coverage for an elderly parent is discontinued, employees and their families are placed in particularly vulnerable positions, where the costs (in terms of time, money, and effort) can be overwhelming. Most of the time these events are a surprise and health benefits have not been selected with these problems in mind. In such cases, employees may appeal for an exceptional response. In the case of Aaron Dufresne, episodic compassion would be expressed if Anna were to somehow help Aaron maintain his relationship with his physician *outside* the existing limits of the health plan.

Episodic compassion may be the most difficult to implement fairly because the standard will be particularly slippery. When we see the same thing over and over, we can be fair by consistently applying a reasonable response. Is surgery for cosmetic reasons covered? No. Is surgery for emergency appendectomies covered? Yes. But by definition, episodic compassion arises in just those cases that defy easy comparisons and simple rules.

The difficulty of applying episodic compassion may tempt us to refuse it altogether: "Let's just be sure we're systematically compassionate and call it good." This, however, would be blatantly unfair. Remember, different cases should be treated differently, and so to pretend that an exceptional case is just like the others is just as unfair as discrimination, or treating a run-of-the-mill case like an exceptional one.

What Is the Business Case for Compassion?

Compassionate benefits design and coverage decisions will cost money—any exception to the usual rules is likely to cost money, in fact. But compassionate decisions (on both the systematic and episodic level) will help retain employees. Showing compassion and taking exceptional care of individuals after a catastrophic event will foster a kind of loyalty and trust that cannot be found in a paycheck or any other office perk. Offering employees diverse benefit options leads to satisfaction by helping employees meet their individual needs. And to top it off, in the first case below, we will see how compassionate decision-making can also lead to higher productivity through efficiently maintaining employee health.

As much as every business should be compassionate, business size plays a significant role in the wisdom of some types of compassionate health coverage decisions. Smaller businesses are in a better position to make individual exceptions—because benefits personnel are more likely to know of the circumstances that might prompt compassionate decision-making. However, these same businesses often lack some of the resources to offer diverse plans and supplemental coverage. Larger businesses will often have the ability to offer more alternative plans and coverage, but it might be harder to make exceptions within these plans consistently. The sheer number of employees in larger businesses can lead to a greater number and frequency of unusual circumstances.

Of course, this is not to suggest that smaller businesses shouldn't offer diverse plans or that larger businesses shouldn't make compassionate episodic decisions. You'll have to make decisions that make sense for your business and your employees. The point is, give your employees as many alternatives as you reasonably can and don't be afraid to make an exception when it's warranted.

Measuring and Balancing Compassion

The appropriate type and number of compassionate decisions for any business will not be easy to define. While everyone should agree that compassionate decision-making is valuable, it is hard to measure compassion. Still, by noting a series of specific actions or activities that indicate compassion, we can accurately describe some individuals or organizations as *generally* compassionate. Specific decisions, of course, are much more difficult to evaluate. Certainly, meeting every employee need and preference would be compassionate, but it is not a sustainable business practice. In the same way, rigidly applying the limits of a health plan may be more efficient in the short run, but it fails to be compassionate and can end up being very costly in the long run.

One of the simple facts—for good or for ill—of having employer-based health coverage is that employers like you are stuck having to balance health coverage decisions and the other interests of the business. That gives you a reason to do a good job in finding high-quality coverage at a reasonable cost, which is something not every employee would be able to do on his own. But it also means that when business is good, it is easier to offer options, consider expanding coverage for better care of the most vulnerable, and even to make exceptions in catastrophic cases. And when business is off, it is harder to do all of these things. To put it starkly, a business that cannot sustain itself cannot offer benefits at all, let alone benefits that follow the Ethical Guidepost of *Compassion*.

Why Wouldn't an Employer Be Compassionate?

In discussing the ethical ideal of compassion with employers, human resources professionals, and consultants, the common objections to thinking about human compassion as a key ethical principle to drive coverage decisions were not surprising. In fact, we've already mentioned the main issues. But here are some of the responses we heard from employers who have succeeded in considering the Ethical Guidepost of *Compassion* in their decision-making processes.

1. *"If I make one exception, my employees will expect it every time."*

This is far and away the most common sentiment that has stopped employers from acting with compassion, even in some very tragic situations. The concern is fundamentally that if you make an exception once, you will automatically become a doormat. This concern is closely related to the worry that employees will become disgruntled if some are granted exceptions to the available benefits, while others are not. These concerns have led some businesses to avoid any compassionate exceptions, even in times of catastrophe.

But this is an overreaction, according to employers who have expressed compassion in their health coverage decisions. In the first place, in most circumstances only a very limited number of employees would, or should, know much about any particular tragic health situation. The opportunity for widespread resentment is very limited. More importantly, though, in cases that really do merit a new interpretation of the rules, no one feels resentment toward the beneficiary. The situation is catastrophic and tragic; otherwise it wouldn't be under review. Finally, if the *process* for making the change is transparent and consistent, employees will recognize that, should they face such a tragic situation, they too will be treated similarly. For example, in several instances, employers have described to us raising the lifetime limit on health insurance coverage because of the experience of one employee. The process entailed rewriting the plan for their particular circumstance—and no employees complained. Instead, those who knew the situation were profoundly grateful and supportive.

2. *"Given an inch, they'll take a mile."*

Because of a concern similar to the one mentioned above, some businesses report limiting the number of plans or the types of supplemental coverage offered to their employees. No matter what kind of alternatives are offered, employees may feel that some other set of options (that's not presently available) would be better than what is available. Once an employer is accommodating about health benefits, employees will expect them to be accommodating about everything, all the time. Though there's no way to avoid all disgruntled employees, offering employees alternatives in their health benefits will satisfy more employees than a single plan.

3. *"Making exceptions to coverage rules is illegal."*

While we cannot offer legal advice, and it is almost certainly true that capricious changes to coverage rules for purposes of favoritism or in the absence of compelling circumstances could lead to legal troubles, reasonable exceptions are fine. The key is to have a good process in place for evaluating exceptional circumstances (such as appeals) and to ensure that this process is consistently followed.

Case Studies

In the two cases for this chapter, we'll look at how systematic and episodic compassion can be demonstrated in health coverage decisions.

Case 1: Cross-Cultural Communications

Pearson, a major pharmacy/convenience chain (with 20,000 employees), has two broad categories of employees: corporate employees and store employees. Not surprisingly, a larger percentage of store employees are poor and fewer have completed schooling compared with corporate employees. A number of the store employees are also ethnic minorities, some of whom learned English as a second language.

Mike Fouts, benefits manager for Pearson, has recently read that communication is a significant barrier in the medical care of minorities and those who learned English as a second language. These groups are also less likely to follow treatment plans for chronic conditions. He doesn't have a way to check closely, but he suspects that this could lead to more sick leave (paid or unpaid), which would negatively affect productivity and store operations. This concern also leads him to worry that perhaps the current health plan is subtly biased in favor of corporate employees.

Mike knows it would be difficult to gather the information to confirm his concerns about productivity and poor health among his ethnic minority employees, but he decides that a system of checks (like having nurses call patients to make sure they under-stand when and how they are supposed to take any prescribed medication) might help alleviate any differences, and it would be helpful for all employees anyway. He's not sure he'll be able to negotiate this with the health plan, but Mike would like to accom-modate store employees' needs so that communication difficulties won't stand in the way of their health and health care.

We should note from the start that Mike Fouts has his atten-tion on compassionate decision-making. By paying specific atten-tion to the vulnerable populations employed by Pearson, he puts himself (and the company) in a position to make compassionate decisions. One sure way to fail to make compassionate decisions is to ignore vulnerable individuals and groups among employees. Simply assuming that everyone in a given company will need the same health care and use it the same way ignores obvious and important differences.

Mike is also taking a compassionate stance regarding the po-tential problems he has identified. Consider that Mike could have chosen to ignore these employees' communication problems and thought of their appropriate use of health care resources as a prob-lem for the store employees to solve themselves. You can almost hear someone say, "If they don't learn how to use the system, that's not *my* fault." But Mike sees his employees' lack of access as a problem, and even if it's not his fault, it's a problem he can do something about. So he is pursuing a systematically compassionate response.

What we can't automatically see in this case is the appropriate next steps. Some options might be to provide interactive help and guidance for employees who speak limited English when they start new treatments. For example, working with health plans and hospitals, it might be possible to negotiate follow-up telephone calls and prescription refill reminders in the employees' native language. More important than the specific details of what he might do, though, is that Mike is making an effort to provide these employees with useful guidance about their health care through their health plan.

While we're not going into detail on what Mike might do to improve health care communication for these employees, it's worth pointing out that some possible strategies wouldn't have to be limited to ethnic minority store employees. In fact, many strategies to improve communication are likely to help all employees understand their health care better.[1] So Mike could hope to improve the health of all his employees by focusing on this especially vulnerable group. And, of course, Mike hopes that through his efforts employees will have fewer days of sick leave because of their better medical care.

Still, we shouldn't pretend that the kinds of initiatives that Mike is considering will be free, or even inexpensive. Depending on the kinds of changes he makes, they could be quite expensive. In this and other cases, some ideas will be too expensive to carry out. But no one will know what they can afford and what they can do until some attempt is made to lay out the options for addressing the special needs of vulnerable groups of employees. Once this evaluation is completed, then it is reasonable to decide what kinds of plans can be realistically implemented.

This case also illustrates that a commitment to compassion in health care coverage decisions can integrate smoothly with the other Ethical Guideposts. Having a transparent process and making it participatory for all employees might alert Mike to particular vulnerable populations, or needs that he had not previously thought about. Consistent health coverage decisions should lead to similarly situated employees getting similar coverage, regardless of whether or not they speak English well—this is certainly a driving concern for Mike. And investing in employee adherence to medical recommendations is sensitive to value, because the value of the benefits offered improves when the employees understand and adhere to treatments that will lead to better health outcomes.

Case 2: CodeRight's Coverage Limits

Cathy Roberts works as an administrative assistant for a small computer design firm, CodeRight, which has seventy-five employees. Cathy suffers from inflammatory bowel disease, for which she takes two medications, mesalamine and metronidazole. A flare-up of her colitis (ulcers in the large intestine) prompted her gastroenterologist to treat her with high-dose prednisone (a steroid), starting at a dose of 60 mg/day for a week, then tapering down slowly over time.

Her benefits through CodeRight exclude psychiatric treatments, which are defined by a list of diagnoses and medications. As a consequence of her steroid therapy, however, she suffered well-known psychiatric side effects. Specifically, she became agitated and had terrible insomnia. The insurance company said it would not cover the sedative medication that was used to treat these problems because these medications are listed as "psychiatric." Despite her physician's appeals to the insurance plan's chief pharmacist and then to the medical director, the claim was denied.

Cathy, with a letter from her physician, approaches CodeRight's owner, Jeff Haines, to ask if there's anything he can do to limit her costs for what she and her doctor describe as routine, nonpsychiatric care.

Would it be fair for CodeRight to help pay for Ms. Roberts' prescription in this case? Mr. Haines is in a difficult spot. Maybe passing the responsibility back to the insurance company would be the easiest thing to do. But the insurance company refused to cover the medicine and has already denied an appeal. In essence, by simply passing the responsibility back to them, Mr. Haines would be refusing to help Ms. Roberts. In one sense, the consistent thing to do would be to refuse to help Ms. Roberts—the plan clearly excludes the prescription drug Ms. Roberts needs. Since other employees with agitation or insomnia can't get coverage for sedatives, an exception should not be made for her. But it would demonstrate compassion to help Ms. Roberts, because she is asking for treatment of the side effects of her other medications and not for treatment of a psychiatric condition. In that sense, it could also be said that her situation is different from other employees who have insomnia for other reasons.

Mr. Haines could also join Ms. Roberts and rechallenge the insurance company's classification of these symptoms as psychiatric. While the insurance company has defined her condition as psychiatric, the case is not so clear. The side effects she suffered were psychiatric in nature, but her physician believes they were entirely due to the prednisone, which she received for her inflammatory bowel disease, a medical condition. Having Mr. Haines' assistance in an appeal might or might not result in a different decision, but we have been told by many employers that when they get involved in appeals, they often have greater success than individual patients do.

It's also possible that Mr. Haines could request clarification on the denial and an estimation of the cost to cover Ms. Roberts' treatment, with an eye towards possibly expanding the coverage.

In the last case, many areas of overlap between compassion and the other four Ethical Guideposts were evident. In this case, though, the guideposts of compassion and consistency at first glance seem to be in conflict. But are they really? The coverage excludes psychiatric conditions, but it doesn't specifically exclude coverage for treatment of psychiatric complications of medical treatment. So allowing coverage for this sort of unusual situation, even it it requires a change in the policy, might not be an inconsistent interpretation. Now that this situation has arisen, it could justify a permanent change, which would also make it clear how these sorts of cases will be handled in the future. A compassionate decision, in any event, would cover the prescription.

Conclusion

This chapter has offered specific steps to follow the Ethical Guidepost of making your decision-making process *Compassionate*. This guidepost is unique, though, in that it helps to think of the other four Ethical Guideposts as being bound together and forming a web of compassion. Because in the end, decisions that are transparent, participatory, consistent, and sensitive to value are very likely to be compassionate decisions. In this sense, because compassion binds together and flows from the other Ethical Guideposts, if all the other Ethical Guideposts are being followed, compassion is a natural result.

At the same time, though, compassion is the Ethical Guidepost that ensures ongoing flexibility in decision-making and that compels attention to the most vulnerable among us. Things change. New situations arise. Unusual needs come up. Catastrophic events occur. Compassion is what encourages all of us to come together and help meet these unpredictable needs.

Note

1. For a number of ideas about improving communication in health care, see the Ethical Force Program's report, *Improving Communication—Improving Care*, available at: www.Ethical Force.org.

▲

Putting It All Together

Ensuring Fair Decisions

R *oark Williams is in charge of designing the health care cover-*
age for Sellers and Sellers, a modestly sized commercial real
estate firm (225 employees). He has recently been charged with
finding ways to save money on the health care benefits package for
the company. Though the company's costs are still reasonable,
they have been steadily rising and will not be affordable in just a
few years. Sellers and Sellers is taking a proactive posture, working
to address the costs of health care coverage before they get out of
hand.

Roark's first step is to conduct a voluntary and anonymous
survey of employees regarding the plans that are currently offered.
As a whole, employees report satisfaction with the care and costs
of the present plans. Nonetheless, when prodded (on the survey),
a number of employees expressed interest in health savings ac-
counts and other plans.

Roark then makes an open call for employee volunteers to
serve on a new committee to consider health care coverage alterna-
tives. Eventually, the committee includes a diverse set of employee
volunteers, who spend several weeks learning about and discussing
health care benefits options. They even spend an afternoon at a

mini-retreat, where they play a board game that highlights some of the coverage choices they might decide to recommend. In the end, the committee recommends keeping the HMO and PPO offerings, but they recommend offering a new health savings account option. The health savings account offers the prospect of reduced premium costs for both the employees and the company. Because the out-of-pocket costs for the company are less from month to month for the health savings account, the committee also recommends that Sellers and Sellers set up health reimbursement accounts for the first portion of the deductible for employees enrolled in the health savings account. This should be an incentive for employees to choose the health savings account.

The committee also addresses a number of other concerns raised by employees on the surveys and in private conversation. For example, some employees have been asking about vision care, and others have asked whether they could get long-term care insurance through work. The committee recommends offering these as options, but without a subsidy from Sellers and Sellers. In the survey, a much larger number of lower pay scale employees said that they hadn't purchased the health insurance. So, to encourage these lower pay scale employees to purchase health insurance, the committee recommends that Sellers and Sellers vary how much it pays toward the cost of health insurance, with lower pay scale employees getting more help. The committee also looks into the quality of care offered by their current health plan, mainly by looking at its scores on the HEDIS® reports. It turns out that another local health plan scores better than theirs on several measures. The committee does not recommend an immediate change, however, because that can be so disruptive. Instead, they decide to investigate how many employees would have to change doctors or hospitals if they made the switch in a future year. In the meantime, they recommend that Roark mention how seriously he and his employees take quality of care, and ask about the HEDIS® scores, when he next meets with the health plan representatives.

Finally, Roark and the committee organize a set of three open *forums to provide employees an opportunity to understand the changes that are being made. Employees were encouraged to submit written questions in advance, but are also allowed to ask questions during the forum. A few days before the open forums, the committee arranges to have a packet delivered to all employees. The packet includes a one-page document that is a side-by-side comparison of all the coverage options that will be available. But the packet also includes more detailed information on each option and it tells the employee how to find out more from the plan or by contacting Roark or the committee.*

In the chapters leading up to this one we've used an opening case to discuss a single Ethical Guidepost. The opening case for this chapter is designed to illustrate all five Ethical Guideposts, and how they can work together.

The Five Ethical Guideposts of Fair Decisions

Transparency

Transparent health coverage decisions are the first step in fair health coverage decision-making. Without transparency, employee participation will be undermined because they lack the information needed to meaningfully contribute. Without transparency, even if your health care coverage decisions are consistent, sensitive to value, and compassionate, your employees won't know that. Because they don't know how these important decisions are made, they will have to imagine what goes into your decisions. And their imaginations might not be as charitable toward you and your motives as you would like.

What's more, failing to be transparent undermines much of the business case for fair health coverage decisions. The reason being fair about health care coverage decisions makes such good business sense (as well as ethical sense, of course) is that employees who know that you are treating them fairly will be more satisfied, loyal, and productive. But if they don't know about the efforts you make to ensure their health benefits are consistent, valuable, and compassionate, then you don't get any of these benefits.

The benefits design process at Sellers and Sellers is fully transparent, from the solicitation of employee volunteers for the committee at the beginning of the process through to the open forums and helpful informational materials at the end of the process. Asking for volunteers cues employees to the evaluation process and potential changes in health care coverage, and the open forums give employees a chance to understand the benefits offered and the changes made.

Participatory

Employee participation in benefits design is pivotal for fair health coverage decisions. Without it, your decisions will be less credible and also of lower quality. Whether it's through committee work, surveys, or just a complaint box, employees bring a perspective that it will be nearly impossible for you to get in other ways. It's true, employees won't always know what they want, they may think they want things that they later decide they don't, and sometimes they want the impossible. But then again, that's true of us all. In the end, employee participation is the only reliable way to inform benefits designers about any problems encountered, the needs that exist, and the expectations employees have of the coverage.

Identifying and then using employee values and priorities in the decision process is the key to participatory decision-making. Sellers and Sellers has done an exemplary job of including employee participation in their benefits design process. The survey and later employee meetings both offered a chance for employees to have meaningful input. While the new committee they established does not have decision-making authority over benefits, Roark takes its recommendations very seriously. As a result, the committee also takes its responsibility seriously. When it comes to difficult decisions, like recommending to change health plans, the group wants to gather more information. Through the participatory process, these employees have become well aware of the trade-offs involved in making health care coverage decisions.

Consistency

Consistent health coverage is a hallmark of fair decision-making. No matter what other features a decision may have, if it's not applied consistently, it won't be seen as fair by employees. Period. In fact, sometimes employees themselves will ask for benefits to be applied inconsistently, or for an inequitable set of benefits—but even their participation in the decision would not make a decision to offer inconsistent benefits a fair decision.

Sellers and Sellers is interested in making sure all employees have consistent access to the health insurance plans they offer. Roark is considering whether to offer a higher contribution for lower pay scale employees, as the committee recommended, but he wants to talk to other employers who've done this first, to see what the long-term effects have been. He also wants to get some feedback on the plan from his higher pay scale managers. Ideally, they should buy into the idea before it is implemented.

Sellers and Sellers are also trying to be equitable in their financial support of various employee choices in another way. They plan to offer a similar level of financial support for premiums (if you chose the standard health plan) or for premiums and deductibles (if you chose the health savings account plan). This was partly to encourage employees to pick the health savings account plan (which costs the company less), but it also made sure that employees who picked the HSA plan got about the same amount of financial support as did those who picked the standard plan.

Sensitive to Value

Depending on whether or not your company self-insures, this Ethical Guidepost could pose the fewest, or the most and the thorniest, direct ethical dilemmas during your decisions about your health coverage package. Most employers try to avoid getting directly involved in decisions about choosing one treatment for coverage versus another for any given medical condition. These are often called "medical necessity" determinations, and they can be extremely complex and demand solid expertise in medicine and other areas. But if you self-insure, it is possible that you will be involved in making these complicated medical decisions. If so, then your responsibilities include making sure the treatments you cover are medically valuable, cost-effective, and also sensitive to individual variations. In chapter 7, we referred to these different aspects of value as *clinical effectiveness*, *cost-effectiveness*, and *personal value*. In sum, treatments that are covered should be clinically and cost-effective, and any side effects (both medical and otherwise) should be ones that employees are willing to accept.

If your company doesn't self-insure, you're much more likely to be at least one step removed from these sorts of direct medical decisions. In that case, your responsibility will be to ensure (through third-party reports like HEDIS® or HealthGrades®) that the insurance company or health plan you use provides high-quality care at a reasonable price. This is a fairly standard business purchasing decision in some ways, but in others it is unique. You will almost certainly be working with a broker to make this decision, and you might find it necessary to hire a consultant to help sort through this information.

Sellers and Sellers is not self-insured, so Roark does not have to make decisions about medical necessity. But their commitment to being sensitive to value is indicated by the committee's attention to the HEDIS® information. It is also reflected in Roark's careful consideration of the priorities and recommendations from the committee. For instance, the health savings account plan was selected, in part, because it was seen as a better value for Sellers and Sellers and their employees.

Compassionate

Sometimes compassion will be the most difficult Ethical Guidepost to follow, because compassionate decision-making can, at first blush, appear to run counter to consistent decisions that are sensitive to value. By making an exception, it can seem as if you're not being consistent or that resources are being spent for less-than-the-usual expected return. But remember, it is fair to treat different cases differently. Making an exception is appropriate in exceptional circumstances.

Even more importantly, health care is a unique purchase compared to most items or services a business buys. In health care, fairness requires special attention to individuals in particularly vulnerable positions. For the same reasons that our communities often spend additional resources on a child who falls down a well, or miners trapped in a collapsed mine, or climbers stranded on a mountaintop, we often devote extra resources to the very ill. We all know that we might be that ill person one day, and we recognize that coming together to help one another says something important about our community. It says that, as a community, we value each other. As a community—whether as Americans, or as citizens of a state, or as members of some smaller community, such as a military unit or the employees of a company—paying special attention to our most vulnerable members is how we show our deepest values; we don't leave people behind.

The health insurance system was established specifically to make sure that when each of us is at our most vulnerable, the resources will be there to help us make it through. Sustaining this sense of communal sharing of risk and responsibility has tangible benefits for any community, including the community of employees in your business.

Sellers and Sellers have shown compassion in a variety of ways, starting with their analysis of the survey data. When they found that lower pay scale employees were less likely to be insured, they acted to alleviate the difficulty faced by these less em-powered employees. When some individuals asked for specific coverage, such as long-term care insurance, they worked to pro-vide it as an option. Though it isn't mentioned in the case, Sellers and Sellers also asked about appeals in the survey, and they main-tain tabs on how the appeals process works at their health plan. Sometimes, they have found that a set of similar appeals marks a problem in the coverage.

Summarizing the Business Case
(Once More, with Feeling)

Making fair health coverage decisions is an important part of mak-ing good business decisions. In the last five chapters, we've seen how each Ethical Guidepost for fair health care coverage decisions contributes to good business. Putting it all together, when your decision-making process is transparent, participatory, consistent, sensitive to value, and compassionate, you put your employees in a position to better understand and appreciate their health care benefits. Even in challenging times, if it is done right, following the Five Ethical Guideposts can help you transform your health bene-fits decisions from a point of contention and conflict into a tool to build a satisfied, loyal, and productive workforce.

Here we want to make another point, too. From the case above, you can see how the Five Ethical Guideposts flow together, one into the next, to make the business case increasingly strong.

Transparent decisions are the baseline—the starting point from which all the other Ethical Guideposts naturally arise. Trans-parency means informing your employees in clear, understandable ways about their coverage and how decisions about coverage are made.

Participatory decisions naturally follow transparency, because as employees learn more they can be more involved and helpful in the process. Employee participation is the only way to ensure that your decisions reflect the most important employee concerns. If you want to craft a health plan that will lead to employee satisfaction, loyalty, retention, and productivity, then you will need to have meaningful employee participation. Without employee participation, you will be flying blind.

Consistent decisions will flow from employee participation, since employees want to be treated equitably. In fact, research has shown that employees who think they are being treated inequitably at work are more likely to call in sick! Similarly, coverage decisions that are transparent and participatory will of necessity be sensitive to value. Participation will ensure that covered services are valued by your employees.

Finally, for the human community, if the process for making decisions is transparent, participatory, consistent, and sensitive to value, it will also promote compassion and flexibility in the exceptional cases where this is needed. Compassion in decision-making around health crises is part of human nature, it's integral to how we think of health insurance, and it is beneficial for the community over the long run. In fact, we heard from several business leaders that, from a business standpoint, being compassionate in the right circumstances can contribute to esprit de corps in a way that is almost impossible to achieve in any other way.

Since the Ethical Guideposts tend to flow together, it is also possible, from a business standpoint, to contemplate a hypothetical business that cares *only* about the immediate bottom line in its health care coverage decisions—ignoring any long-term benefits related to employee satisfaction, loyalty, retention, or productivity. In such a case, the business might, at first, seem to care only about Ethical Guidepost #4: *Sensitive to Value,* because ensuring that coverage decisions are sensitive to value is quite clearly and directly tied to the bottom line. If the business self-insures, this direct correlation is most obvious—inefficient or ineffective coverage decisions cost the business money without any return. The business might as well be throwing money down the drain. This includes covering ineffective treatments or paying to cover treatments that employees won't use. But even if the business doesn't self-insure, its coverage decisions still must be sensitive to value. The company should look for and use those health plans that most effectively and efficiently provide health benefits for its employees; otherwise resources are being wasted.

In either event (whether self-insured or not), if the business's only goal is to ensure that its health benefits are of maximal value, a participatory process will be needed to achieve this. "Value," after all, has to take into account the needs and priorities of the enrollees. Even cost-effectiveness analyses (CEA) must incorporate numerical information on health values in order to make estimates of how cost-effective one service is compared with another in a given population. And once the business needs a participatory process, it also needs to be transparent, because participation without adequate information won't provide useful input.

And so it goes, until the Five Ethical Guideposts have come together again.

In the end, the lesson is that any business that wants to do health care benefits well must pay attention to the ethics of these decisions.

Consistent, but Not Transparent?

Sadly, even though the Five Ethical Guideposts are closely related, there is one Ethical Guidepost that can be present in the absence of the other four. When this happens, it is a tragedy.

Health care coverage decisions can be consistent even if the rest of the guideposts are not followed. But the result is not fairness. In point of fact, it almost certainly will be seen as profoundly unfair by employees.

Consistently applying coverage rules that are misunderstood (because they are not presented in a transparent way), not responsive to employees' needs and priorities (because they are not developed in a participatory fashion), not sensitive to value (because they are not well researched, or are driven by considerations other than effective and efficient health care delivery), or that are not compassionate and flexible in appropriate circumstances, runs a very significant risk of not only being perceived as unfair, but even being seen as mean, stingy, discriminatory, or capricious!

Using Resources like HEDIS®, and Knowing Your Limits

An important part of making fair health care coverage decisions is taking advantage of available resources. One area that often requires the use of outside resources is assessing which health plans can provide the most efficient and effective health benefits for your employees. A key source of this sort of information is the HEDIS® dataset. Sadly, research has shown that even though HEDIS® information is available for free to any employer (see www.health choices.org), relatively few employers use HEDIS®, or even know about it or how to use it.

In addition, your efforts to make fair decisions will probably require frequent collaboration with third parties from other organizations. No matter if you're the owner of a small business or the director of the human resources department in a Fortune 100 company—you can't know everything. Acknowledging this and taking advantage of other resources, including the information provided by colleagues, brokers, or consultants, can be invaluable.

Conclusion

We wrote this book with one thing in mind: When picking health care benefits for their employees, most people, most of the time, try to be fair, and they try to make the best decisions they can with the information they have. Part of this has to do with human nature; we all want to work in a strong and healthy community of employees. But it also has to do with solid business acumen. When it comes to making decisions about health care benefits packages for your employees, making good decisions can really pay off. And making bad decisions can be very costly.

We hope that what we've done in this book is to give you some specific ideas and tools to help you ensure that your decision-making process is as fair as possible. That's why this book includes not only the general Ethical Guideposts for making fair decisions, but also a set of examples and specific steps under each guidepost, to help start you on your way.

Like the quest for ethical perfection in any area, though, the quest for complete fairness is a journey, not a destination. The Ethical Guideposts don't mark the end of the road, but the guardrails. They can help someone on this quest to stay on the path and keep heading in the right direction.

Afterword

At present, the United States spends about 16 percent of its entire gross domestic product on health care. This might be too high or it might be too low, but one thing is certain—it is going up too fast. If we keep up the current rate of growth, by 2050 health care costs would take up 88 percent of the total U.S. gross domestic product![1]

Needless to say, that would be unsustainable. And in fact, current expenditures are already causing real problems. For more than ten years now, we have lamented the fact that our high health care costs are hurting U.S. competitiveness. In May 2006, former President Clinton reiterated this charge, noting that General Motors now pays $1,500 per car for health care.[2] In 2004, the Big Three automakers spent $6.7 billion on retiree health care costs alone. Meanwhile, Toyota's 2005 annual report said that the costs of health care for its retirees "are not material."[3]

And while employers have seen regular double-digit increases in health care costs lately, employees have been feeling the pinch as well. In the last decade, the average annual cost of health insurance premiums for an individual employee has increased from about $2,400 in 1998 to about $3,500 today, after adjusting for inflation. As a result, more and more employees are going without insurance—three million more since 1998, according to a recent Robert Wood Johnson Foundation study.[4]

With this level of decreasing enrollment, many health policy experts believe that if it hadn't been for federal and state efforts to enroll more children in Medicaid in the last ten years, we would have seen very dramatic increases in the numbers of the uninsured.

None of these trends bode well for U.S. businesses, which bear a large part of the costs of caring for the uninsured over the long haul.[5]

We alluded to some of these trends in the early chapters of this book, but in the weeks after we finished writing it, a number of developments, news stories, and press releases have come out that reinforce our message. These developments underline the changing structures and models of health care coverage in the United States, and some of these changes are along the lines we have advocated, including increasing adoption of what we had thought might be our most controversial suggestions.

In this afterword, we'll summarize a few of these recent events, not to change the overall message of the book, but to reinforce the value of and need for the Five Ethical Guideposts—if anything, recent developments make having some ethical guidance even more important than we had originally envisioned.

As we discussed in chapter 4, consumer-directed health plans (CDHP), which are most often high-deductible health plans (HDHP), are becoming more common. For example, Target recently made waves when they announced much broader use of health savings accounts and health reimbursement account, and the possible elimination of their traditional plans.[6] On March 16, 2006, Watson Wyatt released survey results that confirm there is rising interest in this type of coverage.[7] Watson Wyatt reported that the number of companies offering CDHPs has increased four-fold in the last two years and looks to continue increasing in the coming years. The large and midsize businesses surveyed reported mixed results on how CDHPs affect overall health care costs, but they liked CDHPs in part because they were a means to increase employee participation in health care decisions. Further, even though most of the CDHPs for these businesses were HDHPs, the most successful businesses at controlling costs used both financial (like HDHPs) and nonfinancial strategies to increase employee participation. So, as we suggested in chapter 5, one key to cost control and increased employee satisfaction is to bolster employee participation in health benefits decisions.

On March 16, 2006, Chrysler announced plans to index the health coverage premiums of their workers.[8] As we discussed in chapter 6, this is still an unusual move for employers, but it can ensure that employees on the lower end of the pay scale can afford their premiums. As a result, indexing can contribute to consistency in the health benefits provided across an organization. In Chrysler's case, the top executives of the company could see dramatic increases in their premiums (100 percent or more), while those at the bottom of the pay scale will not see any increase, at least initially. It will be interesting to see if Chrysler expands this indexing to co-pays and deductibles as well. In any case, Chrysler is only the most recent example of what seems to be a growing trend among larger companies, to share the cost of health coverage with employees without unfairly keeping lower pay scale employees from affording the premiums.

Another controversial idea we explored in chapter 6 is to even up benefits for medical and mental health services. A number of employers and insurers have been reluctant to do so, for fear that expenses for mental health services could go through the roof. But a recent study in the *New England Journal of Medicine* shows that including mental health coverage as part of managed health care plans does not increase the overall costs of mental health services; in fact, for some plans, costs actually went down![9] We claimed in chapter 6 that parity among mental and physical illness is fair because it supports consistency. This study illustrates the happy fact that parity is also fair because it follows another Ethical Guidepost: It is *Sensitive to Value*.

In another development that is sensitive to value, the University of Michigan announced in March that employees with certain chronic diseases would have their co-pays eliminated for certain medications that have been proven effective.[10] This follows the experience at Pitney Bowes, which we mentioned in chapter 7.[11] When we saw the Michigan press release, we thought other efforts by companies to lower barriers to effective health care services might follow. And indeed, on April 10, 2006, Pricewaterhouse-Coopers released the results of one of their quarterly surveys on employer health insurance trends. They found that today, two out of three larger employers are offering their employees incentives to develop and maintain healthy lifestyles.[12] In addition, two out of five larger employers are providing their employees with health care data to help them make decisions. Both of these results are encouraging. Over the coming months and years, it will be interesting to see the effects of these initiatives: both wellness incentives and the provision of consumer-oriented information. Hopefully, reducing barriers to using effective services will help keep health care costs down, while providing better information will help employees to make better health care and lifestyle decisions.

Stay tuned, and in the meantime, please send us information about your own experiences practicing the Five Ethical Guideposts.

Matthew Wynia, MD, MPH
Abraham Schwab, PhD
Chicago, Ill., May 22, 2006

Notes

1. Morton Kondracke, "Politicians battle as health costs hurt U.S. economy," *Roll Call*, May 4, 2006.

2. C.K. Johnson, "Former president says health care costs hurting U.S. competitiveness," Associated Press State and Local Wire. May 20, 2006.

3. E. Porter, "Japanese cars, American retirees," *New York Times*, May 19, 2006.

4. Robert Wood Johnson Foundation, "Report shows decline in employees accepting health insurance, rising insurance premiums across nation." Available at: http://www.rwjf.org/newsroom/newsreleasesdetail.jsp?id=10408 (accessed May 21, 2006).

5. P. Fronstin, ed., *The Economic Costs of the Uninsured: Implications for Business and Government* (Washington D.C.: The Employee Benefit Research Institute, 2000).

6. C. Serres, "Tough health care medicine for Target workers," *Minneapolis Star Tribune*, May 11, 2006.

7. "Employer interest in consumer-directed health plans growing," Watson Wyatt/National Business Group on Health Survey Finds. Available at: www.watsonwyatt.com/news/press.asp?ID = 15826 (accessed May 21, 2006).

8. M. Maynard, "Chrysler's salaried workers to pay more for health care," *New York Times*, March 16, 2006.

9. H.H. Goldman, R.G. Frank, M.A. Burnam, et al. "Behavioral health insurance parity for federal employees," *New England Journal of Medicine*, 354(13): 2006; 1378–1386.

10. "University of Michigan unveils innovative medication program," Press Release April 24, 2006. Available at: http://www.umich.edu/news/index.html?Releases/2006/Apr06/r042406 (accessed May 21, 2006).

11. "Total value/total return (TM) tells the Pitney Bowes experience: healthier employees translate into a healthier bottom line," PRNewsWire, April 17, 2006. Available at: http://media.prnewswire.com / en / jsp / tradeshows / events.jsp?option = tradeshow& beat = BEAT_ALL&eventid = 1001951&view = LATEST&resource id = 3187226 (accessed May 21, 2006).

12. PricewaterhouseCoopers Press Release, "Two-thirds of large employers now offering incentives to improve employees' health," April 10, 2006. Available at: www.pwc.com/extweb/nc pressrelease.nsf/docid/FD126764F4A20F728525714C0061D9CA (accessed May 21, 2006).

The Expert Advisory Panel on Benefits Determination

*T*he individuals' affiliations are listed for identification only. Individual participation on the Advisory Panel does not imply that the individual endorses or approves of every statement or opinion in this book—only the authors can claim that, so only they can be blamed for any of its faults.

Gail Agrawal
University of North Carolina School of Law

Robert Alpert
United Auto Workers

Mary Jane England
Washington Business Group on Health*

Bruce Jennings
The Hastings Center

*Affiliation at the time of her service on the Expert Advisory Panel. Dr. England is now at Regis College.

Allan Korn
Blue Cross Blue Shield Association

Donald Light
University of Medicine and Dentistry of New Jersey

Russell Massaro
Joint Commission on Accreditation of Healthcare Organizations

Rick Miller
Blue Cross Blue Shield of Tennessee

Thomas Morley
General Motors

James Sabin
Harvard Pilgrim Health Care/Harvard University

Inger Saphire-Bernstein
Blue Cross Blue Shield Association

▲

Steering by the Rearview Mirror

Factors That Shape Employee Health Plans

A Report of Focus Groups
with
Health Plan Purchasers, Brokers, and Consultants

This research was made possible through support provided by:
The Institute for Ethics at the American Medical Association
The Ethical Force Program
and
The Agency for Healthcare Research and Quality

Melane Kinney Hoffmann
Matthew Wynia, MD, MPH
George I. Balch, Ph.D.

This condensed version was produced by Abraham Schwab and Matthew Wynia. The original, full report on the focus groups is available online at www.EthicalForce.org.

Introduction

A critical determinant of the health care many Americans receive is the health plan or plans offered through their place of work. Two-thirds of the workforce, more than 150 million Americans, obtain access to health care through employer-sponsored health plans. Many experts have said that employers, as large-volume purchasers of health plans, have leverage that could be a driving force in the evolution of the health care system.

By extension, employers are an important audience for the consensus reports of the Ethical Force Program, which describe ways in which the health care system should evolve to ensure ethical, high-quality care for all. Therefore, at the beginning of its work on fair coverage decisions in 2000, the Ethical Force Program decided to explore the processes by which employers select plans, the factors that influence their selection, and what ethical issues, if any, come into play.

To conduct this research, the Ethical Force Program contracted with Balch Associates, a social marketing research consulting firm in Chicago, to design, conduct, and analyze focus groups among employer health benefits decision-makers. After a first set of focus groups with employers had been completed, the Ethical Force Program and the federal Agency for Healthcare Research and Quality (AHRQ) sponsored another set of focus groups, this time with health insurance brokers and consultants, with whom employee decision-makers virtually always confer when making decisions about health benefits.

This appendix provides a synopsis of the results from both sets of focus groups, focusing on results from this research that are reflected in the rest of the book.

Research Methods

Altogether, we conducted a total of ten focus groups. First, six focus groups were conducted among employer decision-makers.

Next, four focus groups were conducted among brokers and consultants. All of the groups were conducted using a computer-assisted telephone system, which allows many busy, geographically dispersed people to participate from their offices and homes around the country. Each discussion lasted about ninety minutes and was facilitated by an experienced focus group moderator, George I. Balch, PhD, of Balch Associates. All discussions were audiotaped and transcribed with participants' advance permission.

Focus Groups of Benefits Decision-Makers

We planned the composition of the focus groups to ensure that we explored a range of situations and viewpoints. The six health plan decision-maker focus groups had eight or nine participants each, all of whom had primary responsibility for selecting the health benefits plan for their organizations. Two groups represented small companies (10–99 employees), two groups represented medium-size companies (100–999 employees), and two groups came from large companies (1,000 or more employees). All participants offered at least one health plan, and for the two large company focus groups, participants were screened to make sure we included at least two participants in each group whose companies' employees were represented in contract negotiations by one or more labor unions.

Focus Groups of Brokers and Consultants

During the first set of six focus groups among employer health plan decision-makers, it became clear that all of them—whether with small, medium, or large companies—relied heavily on the advice of health insurance brokers and/or consultants. Thus, we conducted a second set of four focus groups among health benefits brokers and consultants.

Three of these four focus groups were conducted with brokers whose primary business is commercial coverage (rather than indi-

vidual coverage), and a fourth group consisted of health care benefits consultants. Each group had nine participants. Of the three
commercial coverage broker groups, two were with brokers who
deal primarily with small companies (2–50 employees), and the
third was with brokers who deal primarily with midsize companies
(51–999 employees). Large businesses of 1,000 or more employees
typically use the services of specialized consultants from brokerage
or consulting firms, and thus the fourth group was comprised of
these types of firms.

Questions for the Focus Groups

Participants in all the focus groups were told that the discussion
would include questions as to (1) who—besides themselves—was
involved in decisions about changing health plans, (2) what information did they use in making decisions about what health plans
to offer, and (3) what role, if any, did issues relating to quality,
ethics, and values play in the selection process.

Findings

Although much about choosing health plans has changed since
2000, this research provided the Ethical Force Program with useful
information about the individuals that participate in selecting
health plans to offer employees. It also shed light on the typical
sequence, priorities, and key sources of information they use during the selection process.

The Players and Their Roles

The two types of professionals studied—the decision-makers inside organizations and the outside brokers and consultants who
counsel them—reflected parallel thinking about the roles and relative influence of various groups in the decision-making process.

The Insiders

Participants in the employer focus groups were themselves key insiders in the health plan selection process—indeed, this is why they were selected for inclusion in the study. For instance, many participants in the employer groups were top human resources personnel in their companies, while others were very senior managers, such as owners, CEOs, or presidents of companies. All participants appeared to agree that *human resources managers,* other *top management,* and *employees* each had important roles to play in the health plan selection process. In some companies, *unions* were a significant factor, as well. The specific titles, roles, and responsibilities of these various players differed, but followed some predictable patterns.

Top management review: Participants in employer focus groups who were not in top management themselves reported that they usually receive or gather and then analyze information from several sources, though especially from brokers and consultants, then form a recommendation for top management or sometimes for an executive board.

Employee influence: Feedback from employees may be a major factor in decisions to change health plans. Complaints were the most common form of feedback and carried the most weight. Formal surveys quantifying employee experiences or satisfaction with health plans were uncommon in 2000, even among large companies, though some employers held informal meetings at which employees could provide feedback on their health plans. On the other hand, some participants reported that their companies had formal policies against obtaining quantitative information about employees' experiences with their health plan(s), fearing that gathering such information might create unrealistic expectations for expanded or changed benefits.

We have a policy against surveys because it tends to create . . . anticipation for change on the part of the employee.

A few employers kept a formal complaint log, but most did not. Participants suggested that although they are concerned about all complaints, some complaints carry more weight than others.

> *The [complaints] that will carry the most weight are maybe people that are a little higher up the food chain, but the ones that I take most seriously are when I'm hearing volume.*

In what may be the most general pattern of our findings—a pattern that will repeat itself throughout the remainder of this report and from which the report draws its title—not a single participant in the employer focus groups reported any form of *prospective* employee input into which health plans to offer. At the time of these focus groups, all employee input appeared to be retrospective, based upon complaints about negative experiences with health plans.

Brokers and Consultants

All of the employer decision-makers with whom we spoke—from human resources professionals and benefits specialists in medium and large companies to presidents, owners, and office managers in small companies—reported that they used brokers and/or consultants to help them decide what benefits to offer.

In some cases, in particular among smaller employers, the broker or consultant served as the equivalent of a human resources staff. One broker characterized these relationships as follows:

> *Depending on the size—those [clients] that don't really have a designated human resources person—they're oftentimes counting on their broker as their human resources person. Kind of like outsourcing pieces of human resources.*

Especially in smaller companies, "outsourcing" human resource/benefits decisions to a broker or consultant may make sense because the client typically has little or no human resources background. One participant in an employer focus group said:

I don't have the time or the expertise to know everything . . . going on, that's what you hire the consultant for, and so we buy their expertise to help guide us.

Another employer described a situation in which the broker did time-consuming background work for which the client had neither the time nor the expertise.

That's one of the reasons I use a broker, just to simplify the process, to let them do all that research . . . I have a lot of confidence in my broker.

Statements of trust in brokers and consultants were common. Some participants described relationships in which brokers were in a position to establish priorities and define issues for the client:

I utilize my broker all year 'round and I have the broker analyze the data on a monthly basis and then report to me on the information that's meaningful to me.

Additionally, employers often had their brokers or consultants manage day-to-day health plan issues.

When we've had problems in the past with difficult claims or something, I've pushed it off on the broker and let his staff basically do the footwork and slug it out with the carrier.

Brokers and consultants observed that their level of influence appears to increase as they establish trust with clients over several years of annual health plan renewal processes.

When we go into a [client] group that is brand new, we have one role and that is to really to sell ourselves to build up a relationship, build up a trust factor. And so I see that constantly changing, from one of being more of an information gatherer at first and selling ourselves, to really being part of the actual decision at the end when we've had a group for several years.

Brokers and consultants, despite being "outsiders" to the organizations, had substantial influence in the health plan selection process even at the largest employers. Therefore, insurance brokers might wield more influence in evaluating and selecting health plans than policy makers realize.

What Information Is Used in Deciding to Change Health Plans?

Regardless of their size, sophistication, or resources, all participating employer decision-makers and the brokers and consultants who advised them started at a common point: The most fundamental decision is whether to make a change each year or to stay with the current health plan(s) or carrier(s). (All participants reviewed their health benefits packages annually.) Although an outsider might expect that this annual decision creates an opportunity to "comparison shop" or negotiate improvements to the plan, most employer participants indicate that changing plans is time consuming, expensive, and generally burdensome; thus they only undertake a change if the current plan or plans pose serious problems. In short, they would prefer to "stay put" if there is no compelling reason to change. The discussion revealed that the decision to change is usually triggered by three key factors: cost, employee dissatisfaction, or when a health plan "changes the rules of the game" in midstream.

Cost Increases

If the plan or carrier quotes a substantial cost increase, employers look elsewhere. Consultants and brokers mentioned cost

BROKER COMMISSIONS: CONFLICT OF INTEREST OR ROUTINE RISK?

In the employer groups, there was rarely any mention of the fact that brokers, who are usually paid a commission by the carriers or plans they sell to clients, could have a financial incentive to recommend some health plans to their clients over other plans, potentially creating a conflict of interest. Generally, among small and medium-size employers, for whom brokers are a primary and sometimes sole source of information, there appeared to be little cognizance of any conceptual or practical distinction between a broker (who is paid a commission by the health plan) and a consultant (who is paid by the employer). Larger employers were for the most part aware of the differences between brokers and consultants, but were only modestly concerned about any conflict of interest.

I feel that consultants are more independent [but] I have worked with some good brokers [too] and I think they have done a good job for us. But I think you have to be a lot more vigilant and really be cautious that they're [brokers] not just staying with the same companies all the time.

For their part, while brokers agreed among themselves that the commission paid by a plan should not be the first or most important consideration in reviewing it, they freely acknowledged the existence of a conflict of interest in commission payments. Most had a strong sense of professionalism about their work, holding that the best interests of their clients would trump any personal concerns about commissions.

I don't think any of us ask what the commission is before we make a decision to sell a product. But at the end of the day we are in the business to survive . . . But I don't think any of us . . . would use that as the deciding factor on what to show our clients.

Other brokers and consultants reported that commissions had a stronger influence:

I would like to make a comment that nobody has said anything about yet but I think we all think it . . . at least in the back of our minds . . . quite honestly, I'm running a business, not just selling insurance, and I've got to be able to make a profit on a case. So that's going to have an influence on the company that I market.

I think that this thing we've talked about . . . commissions . . . has really not been an issue except in the last year. And I think it will become an issue in how we present and how we recommend. Because I personally have never thought about commissions. I just work and like to deal with people. But boy, I'm looking at it close.

This apparently growing ethical dilemma had some brokers moving more toward consulting arrangements and away from commissions. One broker said:

One of the things we have been realizing is . . . that yes, different insurance companies are starting to squeeze. And quite frankly, from our side we are moving a lot from the commission-based to the consultant-based and just going into our customers and saying 'Take us out of the loop . . . cut us a check, be it at the beginning of the year or monthly, however you would like to do it.'

It is noteworthy that brokers and consultants held materially divergent views from their clients on the issue of conflicts of interest. While many brokers and consultants were concerned about such conflicts—so much so that some were changing their practices to avoid them—their clients, employer decision-makers, assumed that any conflict was minimal and could be kept in check, if it existed, simply by requiring brokers to bring them multiple plans to compare.

as a main reason that their clients became motivated to investigate alternatives.

I'm finding that given the cost increases, access . . . is less important and how a health plan is fundamentally managing medical costs is more important.

Employee Dissatisfaction

Employee dissatisfaction—with customer service, quality of care, or claims processing—was a common reason for initiating a change in health plan offerings. As previously noted, employers usually evaluated dissatisfaction by volume of employee complaints, which they measured informally and retrospectively.

Employee satisfaction would not really enter into choosing a plan. Dissatisfaction might lead us to drop a plan.

Both employer benefits managers and insurance brokers often found themselves drawn into the situation when employees had trouble with claims. In fact, for many of them, employee complaints consumed much of the time they devoted to managing health benefits; consequently, they reported a very strong incentive to see such problems minimized.

This past year . . . we had a significant amount of problems
with our health care provider, and we switched this year
. . . I spent a great deal of my time chasing down people's
claims and things like that, that were not getting paid. So
I was motivated.

A consultant to large companies captured it this way:

When you think about what the purchaser wants, it is for
the [employee] to be able to have a decent relationship so
that . . . there's a zero whine factor.

Changing the Rules

In addition to cost and customer service, another primary reason for changing the health benefits package was in response to
a significant change in procedures and/or regulations. Some such
changes were related to costs or customer service, but others were
not—they had more to do with simply maintaining stability. For
example, the plan might alter its network of participating clini-
cians or hospitals, or it might dramatically alter co-payments, or
the scope of services it offers. When such changes occur, the effect
is often seen as detrimental.

We were . . . asking what kinds of things might trigger a
decision to start to look into other options, and . . . [one]
is when the insurance providers start to change the rules of
the game.

Where Does This Information Come From?

When deciding whether to keep or drop a health plan, employer
decision-makers and their brokers and consultants were primarily
concerned with three factors—cost, member (dis)satisfaction, and
stable rules. Because of this, they said they looked for information
that might give them insights into these topic areas, and they val-

ued some types of information more than others. Apart from employee complaints, as mentioned above, we asked about several other possible sources of information.

Standardized Accreditation and Performance Information

Most of the employer focus group participants do not look at the information provided in independent, quantitative "report cards," which often reveal employee satisfaction with a plan across different populations as well as other information about how the plan has performed. Such report cards are provided by some state insurance commissions, by regional business coalitions, and by national independent, nonprofit organizations, such as HealthGrades®, the National Committee for Quality Assurance (NCQA), and the Joint Commission on Accreditation of Healthcare Organizations (JCAHO). NCQA, for example, compiles HEDIS® data (the Health Plan Employer Data and Information Set), which evaluates health plans across a broad range of key quality indicators, such as member satisfaction, disease management processes, immunization rates, and some health outcomes. In addition, formal accreditation by organizations such as NCQA or JCAHO is based on a large number of quality-of-care and performance criteria. Thus, health plans that are accredited have gone through a standardized screening process to ensure their quality.

Few employer focus group participants were even aware of the availability of such information. Only two of the fifty-two employers participating in the discussion had investigated health plan accreditation, and one was because the company was interested in procuring accreditation for its self-insured plan.

As with accreditation information, few employers were aware of HEDIS® scores or comparable performance evaluations, fewer participants had ever seen or used them, and even fewer found them helpful. Most who were aware of the data said they found the data confusing.

*[HEDIS® scores] were actually included in the package
that the healthcare provider provided to our employees for
that particular carrier, . . . and it raised a lot of questions
with our employees, as to how they were scored and how
do they compare . . . I almost wish they wouldn't have put
it in there.*

Some participants were skeptical of the value of such report cards,
assuming that health plans can easily manipulate the evaluation
process.

*We started looking at that two years ago and what we
found was that the ones with the best HEDIS® ratings had
the worst employee satisfaction. Most of their HMOs have
great HEDIS® scores and the worst reputations with their
employees. . . . [W]hat we've deduced from this is that . . .
they're very adept at satisfying the HEDIS® criteria, but in
the bottom line, in delivering the quality product to the
employees, it's not the same.*

One employer participant reflected a different point of view, however, reporting a positive experience using a regional report card
produced by the Vermont Health Alliance.

*We look basically at the report card . . . They do an
extensive survey here in the state of Vermont for the
managed care programs and the preferred provider
programs and we really take a good hard look at the
results of those . . . They survey the employers and the
employees that are covered and they come out with huge
results. It's everything. It's service. It's the network. It's
the care the 'insureds' are receiving from the providers.
Whether they feel they're getting the care they need or they
are just being shuffled around. . . . So there's a lot of
information that goes on it. And we have to listen to that*

and look at that because our employees are very up on that
information.

Brokers and consultants reaffirmed employers' general lack of understanding or interest in using accreditation and performance data. They report that this unfamiliarity is more common among small companies, whereas large companies, of 1,000 or more employees, are more likely to be aware of quality ratings and to use them. Smaller companies rarely ask about NCQA accreditation, and they ignore the information if brokers present it, relying more on what the broker ultimately recommends.

I try to present that information [accreditation status] to
my groups because this was a big deal here a couple of
years ago. It was one of the competing factors between
some of the companies, as far as who's accredited . . . And
so I try to take that in but I agree with the others, my
groups don't look at them. They don't really care about it.

Some brokers and consultants believe NCQA accreditation is a fundamental requirement, particularly as a safeguard for their smaller clients.

I won't even do business with a company that isn't
[accredited] . . . and has lousy HEDIS® scores. Because
our health insurance marketplace is so tentative at this
moment, we have carriers that are leaving . . . Now to offer
somebody . . . to seriously offer that to a fifty and under
[client] . . . I really hesitate and probably nine times out of
ten don't show them to my clients.

Other brokers and consultants, however, do not place much weight on accreditation.

It may be important for the larger employer who has
multi-state facilities . . . I don't mean to say that the

NCQA accreditation is not, or HEDIS® reports is [sic] not a viable mechanism for judging one health plan versus another. [But] I . . . also try to find out what the targeted loss ratio is of the carrier . . . So I don't necessarily put a lot of credence in NCQA.

Some brokers and consultants specifically mentioned that under some circumstances they would recommend a plan that was not accredited. They believe that even if a plan has been refused accreditation, there may be a range of mitigating factors that outweigh this single factor.

I think you have to look a little farther than just accreditation. I mean that's very nice but you want to go on track record. If this company—you're dealing with them—have always paid claims and given service on a timely basis, that's someone you want to deal with. Because they may not have a sticker on their wall but they're doing what they're supposed to be doing and that's really the most important thing.

Not only were some employer health plan decision-makers unfamiliar with NCQA accreditation and HEDIS® scores, several brokers and consultants were also unfamiliar with HEDIS® and NCQA:

BROKER PARTICIPANT 1: *Very few, if anybody, at least in South Carolina, brings up "HEDIS®" or "NCQA."*

BROKER PARTICIPANT 2: *Thanks for saying that, because I didn't even know what that was.*

BROKER PARTICIPANT 1: *I have to claim ignorance . . . I don't even know what [HEDIS® scores] are.*

BROKER PARTICIPANT 2: *Thank you . . . neither do I.*

BROKER PARTICIPANT 3: *I have . . . been in this business nineteen years and I'm totally unfamiliar with it.*

Other Measures of Quality

If so many health benefits decision-makers do not use standardized quality-assessment tools, and/or do not value the quality measures these assessments capture, then how might they define and assess quality?

Unlike the primary focus of accreditation and most HEDIS® measures, participants did not frame health plan quality in terms of technical proficiency, such as appropriate use of medical procedures, outcomes, or meeting targets for prevention, diagnosis, and treatment of disease. Instead, they tended to focus on delivery issues, such as access to specific providers or services, customer service, and a notion of value based on level of access and service relative to cost.

Access: Doctors and Hospitals in the Network and Prompt Referrals to Specialists

The choice of physicians and hospitals available within a network is inextricably linked to quality in the minds of employers reviewing health plans. For those who can only offer one plan, they strongly prefer to offer one that includes the "best" providers available.

I would have to say that our first consideration is always hospitals on the panel and the doctors and certain medical groups.

Brokers and consultants also reported that "keeping the same doctor" is a critical issue for their clients, not only for the comfort and convenience of all employees, but for concern over clinical issues involving continuity of care in complex cases.

They listen to price, which I think is the main thing. And then 'Is my doctor on the plan?' being the second thing.

The topic of access to care also encompasses timely referrals to specialists and the ability to use "Centers of Excellence" for complex procedures and treatments. Prompt access to specialists is considered an integral part of quality of care.

> *When people say quality of care, they want to know how quickly they will get a referral to a specialist. And will it be weeks waiting? At one point, a few years back, at one of the HMOs, it was weeks before they would get a referral.*

Information About Customer Service

When benefits managers and their brokers and consultants talk about customer service, most often they are referring to employee interactions with the carrier or claims administrator about payment and processing of claims and dealing with the health plan or carrier on the phone. They want "friendly" systems and consistency.

> *The thing that we look for as far as customer service is the prompt payment of the claims and the fact that when somebody calls in, if they get a different person each time they call in, they're getting the same information.*

Participants recognize that poor service can lead to dissatisfaction even with a prestigious plan or carrier. When this occurs, it causes problems for the manager and the broker, who may have to spend time with the carrier trying to work it out.

> *What's their customer service like? . . . that would be key. Because if you have a client that purchases a plan and they purchase it just for price or because their doctor is in it . . . and the customer service isn't there . . . The broker is unhappy because they're getting multitudinous phone calls from a carrier that should be paying their claims. The*

client is unhappy. The employer is unhappy. And the employee is unhappy. It just makes for a lousy situation.

Information About Value

Brokers and consultants who work with larger organizations of 1,000 or more employees were most likely to introduce the concept of "value" into the purchase discussion. The concept was viewed as finding an appropriate balance between cost control and quality of care, yet few felt they had successfully found ways to measure value.

> *What we're finding is our more sophisticated buyers are coming to realize that oftentimes quality has a direct influence on cost. In other words, their first focus may be cost, but as you work with it or as they become more aware of what is really happening they understand that the quality of what they're getting, the quality of service, is definitely affecting their cost.*

Those who contributed to this discussion reported frustration on the part of their clients that it is difficult to measure value in health care.

> *Corporations are very comfortable with the trade-off between cost and quality. When they try to put it, though, within the same kind of framework in which they purchase goods and services the corporation needs, they find themselves extremely frustrated dealing with health care because the metrics we use for quality . . . satisfaction or accreditation or even to some extent HEDIS® are very difficult to translate into anything meaningful to the corporation.*

Information About Cost and Price

Cost, along with related issues such as rate stability and discounts, is of critical importance to the employer decision-makers and the brokers and consultants who advise them. An increase in cost is often the catalyst to consider changing plans, or to consider one that may not have been in the mix. Brokers and consultants consistently confirmed this.

> *I have found that price is very important. It's that bottom line. There are times when I want to try and offer them a better carrier that will cost them more but they always go down to the bottom line. So many of the smaller companies are limited on their budgets. So this is what they have to look at.*

Most consultants and brokers, however, expressed concern over too much emphasis on cost control, based on previous experience that a carrier who offers extremely low prices cannot provide the quality and service clients expect.

> *I'm not going to sell the low bidder. We typically throw out the low bidder from our evaluation and don't even offer it to the client.*

Some consultants and brokers went further, cautioning their clients that choosing the lowest-cost provider is a bad business strategy. Several were adamant that they would not work with clients whose top criterion is low cost.

> *We take business by referral only and we ask them up front if price is [their] primary concern. And if they say 'yes' we'll refer them to another agent.*

> *We take quotes from carriers we will not deal with and I'll tell the group up front that XYZ has lower quotes than I'm showing you and if you want to pursue that I'll recommend an agent that will sell it to you.*

Another important aspect of cost is rate stability. Brokers and consultants are on their guard against plans that offer a low premium as a "come-on" to start a contract year, but find loopholes to raise rates midyear.

Another thing that I look at for companies . . . is rate stability. Rates are important going in, but if they're going to get rate increases every six months . . . and there are carriers that do that . . . I don't even want to go there.

Information About Financial Stability

Financial stability of the plans under consideration is a major concern, because it influences the ability of the carrier or plan to stay in the market, to pay claims, to pay physicians and other providers, and ultimately to provide the agreed-upon coverage.

Stability is a big thing . . . some carriers aren't committed to the group marketplace . . . and they're in it for a few years . . . then they're out and then they're back in again. Are you going to have a client that is in the hospital when they decide to bail?

Some brokers and consultants believe that given the lack of predictability in the health care delivery market, the most dependable predictor of financial stability is longevity.

Somebody said . . . that they wouldn't do business with a company that was less than a year old. We won't do business with a plan that is less than three years old. And there are carriers that are in and out of the market with different plans and we won't touch them because of that.

Information About Provider Payment Structures, Services Provided, Network Stability, and Other Considerations

Several other issues were occasionally raised in the discussion, and although they were not raised as primary considerations, each one was considered a potentially important factor in the overall decision about health benefits. In the negative, each could become a determining factor.

Participants expressed a moderate level of concern that payment structures for practitioners dictated by managed care organizations or carrier contracts might directly influence clinical care. Some participants mentioned specific cases in which plan restrictions caused primary care physicians to refrain from referring to a specialist when they should have, or to withhold treatment that was not covered until or unless certain administrative requirements could be met. They believed these occurrences were rare, and were outraged when they occurred.

In general, participants believe that payment structure conflicts eventually reveal themselves in negative ways.

> But I think there are symptoms [of payment arrangements that conflict with patient care] that show up. For instance, when the capitation amounts are too low that's when you get perhaps greater concern about physicians not acting in the best interest of the patient. That's when you definitely see physician reaction and physician turnover in the network . . . Those are . . . closely linked.

In discussing factors considered aside from cost and customer service, employers frequently talked about the need to keep their benefits on par with their competitors in order to attract and retain employees. Although this was not generally a primary consideration, several employers in every group mentioned it as important and reported that they occasionally investigate the benefit offerings of other companies in their industry.

Ethical Issues Were Not Directly Considered in the Process

The Ethical Force Program, the sponsor of this research, set out to explore many aspects of the health plan selection process in part to illuminate what role ethical considerations might play in these decisions. Notably, most such issues, when raised as issues of ethics *per se*, were not considered to be of obvious importance to either employers or brokers and consultants, nor were they viewed as influencing factors in selecting health plans or determining a health benefits package.

Ethical Issues

When pressed to describe ethical issues that might arise in health plan selection, participants tended to mention obvious ethical transgressions in very black-and-white terms, such as *intentional contract violations* or *fraud*. Examples included health plans trying to get out of paying claims, delaying payment, or denying appropriate treatment; providers overcharging or filing fraudulent claims; or either party violating confidentiality of patient information. They made it clear that, while they believe these types of violations to be very rare, any such type of ethical violation would be totally unacceptable to them.

> *If I ever thought that I was dealing with a plan that wasn't ethical, I don't care what it would offer, I would be somewhere else.*

When pressed by the moderator to explore the possibility of more nuanced ethical issues, decision-makers thought of the ethics of how a health plan operates, with two main areas demonstrating potentially unethical business practices: 1) extremely unresponsive customer service (delayed, inconsistent, or insensitive), and 2) intentionally withholding appropriate care or cutting corners in the quality of care to contain costs. Several decision-makers had experienced these kinds of unethical practices and had had to drop the offending plans.

Fairness of the Appeals Process

The fairness of appeals processes available to patients who want to contest plan decisions, such as nonpayment of claims or

denial of diagnostic testing, procedures, or treatments, was not
raised as an ethical issue by the employer participants. When specifically prompted by the moderator, employers replied that they
assumed their brokers would weed out any carrier with a dubious
appeals process or questionable track record in this area. In fact,
they would much rather avoid appeals to begin with, by avoiding
the events that lead up to the appeals process. Unfortunately, as
mentioned before, they had little proactive information to help
them avoid any problematic plans.

> *I think we need to know this [payment of claims track
> record] up front. Now whether their appeals process is 100
> percent, I don't know that you need to know that much,
> but you do need to know that [if] this company isn't
> paying their claims, you . . . want to stay away from them.*

Brokers and consultants, on the other hand, often considered the
appeals process to be an important feature of plans; they also assumed that most plans have a fair process. But some brokers and
consultants had experiences that caused them to be more circum-
spect.

> *We won't sell a carrier that is not going to pay their claims
> or aren't even going to talk to us about why they're not
> paying.*

One aspect of the "fairness" issue that came up was the need to
make exceptions to stated policy and procedures for individual
employees under extraordinary circumstances. Most employers
felt that it was undesirable to make "exceptions," because it puts
the company at risk of being perceived as unfair, being open to
pressure from high-level employees, and even breaking the law.
However, several participants reported individual situations in
which they helped employees get benefits not covered by the plan
when wrenching health crises arose. They prefer to describe these

incidents as being "flexible" with the rules rather than as "exceptions."

> *I think you cannot make exceptions . . . If you have made*
> *an exception then suddenly that becomes your new plan*
> *provision. However, I do believe in liberal interpretations*
> *where possible. And I like to see a liberal definition of*
> *things like 'medical necessity' or 'experimental and*
> *investigational,' that sort of thing.*

Conclusions

From 2000 until today, health care has remained a top concern for all Americans—for individuals, companies, activists, policy experts, elected political leaders, and the millions who work in or interact with the health care system. Health care costs have continued to spiral upward and a growing number of Americans have lost access to health insurance. At the same time, many concerns about the quality of care have arisen, and demands for accountability are growing.

Against this backdrop, public discussion has often focused on the potential power of purchasers in our market-driven system, in hopes they might have an effect on system evolution. To many observers outside the process, it seems that those who select health plan options for hundreds or even thousands of employees should use their substantial purchasing power to negotiate for better value for their company at the very least, and perhaps more optimistically, to use their volume buying leverage to drive system change. But as we examined the reality of most health benefits decision-makers in 2000, this impression was more the exception than the rule. All segments of the health plan decision-maker teams we studied—from small to large companies, from employer to broker and consultant, from a variety of industries and geographic locales—appeared to be struggling just to provide adequate benefits while keeping cost and employee complaint levels minimized.

As of 2000, among these employers, all were making decisions that profoundly affected their employees, and they were aided greatly by brokers, but they had very little prospective information either on what their employees wanted or on the quality of the health plans they selected. Other than cost, the information that most affected actual selection decisions was retrospective: namely, the volume and types of beneficiaries' complaints over the past year. In sum, the main information that employers used most often could be distilled to two key sources: 1) a broker's recommendation, and 2) an informal assessment of employee complaints.

The best available prospective information on health plan quality, which one might hope would predict complaints or lack thereof, probably comes from accreditation reports and other report cards. But most employers were not aware of these resources, and those who were familiar with them saw them as fuzzy, unreliable, or not addressing the most important issues. For employers making health plan selection decisions, driving while staring into the rearview mirror may not be safe—but when the windshield is foggy, it might seem to be a reasonable choice.

The fundamental roles and responsibilities of the players are interesting. On the one hand, employees generally had little direct input into choosing which plan(s) they might be offered, except through their complaints. On the other hand, outside brokers and consultants were extraordinarily influential. Employers relied on them heavily and had great confidence in their expertise and advice.

The most important aspect of the employer-broker relationship seemed to be the trust many employers placed in their brokers and consultants. They assumed that brokers and consultants were thoroughly checking every potential carrier on quality of care measures, network stability, and high ethical standards. Employers did not worry about these issues or ask about them, because they assumed that their broker would have studied them and screened out any poor performing plans. The discussions with brokers and consultants cast doubt on this assumption, however, as they reported a lack of reliable information on these dimensions. On the other hand, the brokers recognized the trust placed in them, and when they became aware of ethical or quality problems in a plan, they saw it as their responsibility to point this out to employers or to not offer such plans.

Many, but not all, brokers and consultants considered standardized industry data from accreditation and report cards (such as HEDIS®) to be state-of-the-art and essential to their work. While they acknowledged their limitations, they used these standardized data sets regularly in making their recommendations. Brokers and consultants also made use of myriad other formal and informal resources and tools to help form their opinions. For instance, many considered how long a plan had been in the market and avoided new plans, even if they offered low-ball pricing. Some routinely avoided the lowest-priced plans for fear of instability and poor quality. And one of their most respected resources was professional peers, with whom they exchanged information at national conferences and regional or local meetings of business coalitions or professional associations.

Even with so much discussion about ethical issues in the health care arena in 2000, including extensive media coverage of related state and federal regulations (related to fraud and privacy, for example), most of these health benefits decision-makers assumed that all parties in the health care delivery system are ethical until proven otherwise, and that considerations of ethics were therefore not relevant in distinguishing between health plans. As a result, "ethical" concerns *per se* did not usually come into play for most of these decision-makers. On the other hand, when they became aware of ethical issues, they were of profound importance—on those occasions when expectations of ethical action were not met, they acted swiftly and decisively to drop plans or carriers.

This point merits emphasis in respect to the present book: According to these focus group participants, when ethics came into

the picture, though it happened rarely, it was decisive. The serious-
ness with which the participants took ethics in health care, once it
was raised as an issue, suggests that the opportunity exists to add
ethics as a new element in decision-making about health care benefits. The process can only be enriched by this addition.

Selected Resources

"Selected Resources" is a loaded term. There are innumerable books, journals, articles, Web sites, and other resources on how to evaluate and select benefits. We had to narrow it down somehow. In the brief list that follows, we've stuck to just those resources that have been especially useful in our research for this book and that specifically focus on health benefits. You won't see some of the classic books on employee benefits here, not because they aren't very helpful—they are—but because you're probably already familiar with them and they don't focus specifically on *health care* benefits. We've also tried to narrow the list by looking for those resources that have something to say about ethics and the values that might, or should, come into play in selecting health benefits.

First, there are literally thousands of published journal, magazine, and newspaper articles that are relevant in one way or another to ethics and choosing health care benefits. A few of these have been referenced in the book. Because it would be so hard to pick just the best or most relevant among these thousands of articles, in this list of resources we are going to simply omit mentioning any of them, with one exception. One journal article must be mentioned here—and mentioned first—because it is the article on which much of this book was based.

Matthew K. Wynia, Deborah Cummins, David Fleming, Kari Karsjens, Amber Orr, James Sabin, Inger Saphire-Bernstein, and

Renee Witlen."Improving Fairness in Coverage Decisions: Performance Expectations for Quality Improvement," *The American Journal of Bioethics*, 4: 2004; 1–14.

In this concise version of the consensus report on fair coverage decisions, the authors briefly lay out the Five Ethical Guideposts and more than fifty specific ways to measure whether organizations are following them. In addition, in the same issue of the *Journal* there are a number of very interesting commentaries on the consensus report from leading ethicists and policy makers. The full version of the consensus report is available at www.EthicalForce.org.

General Resource Books

We drew from a large number of general reference-type books in our research for this book. The following were among the most helpful.

Kongstvedt, Peter. *The Managed Health Care Handbook*, 4th edition. Sudbury, Mass.: Jones and Bartlett Publishers, 2001.

This rather hefty tome is designed to help employers, policy makers, and managed care executives better understand and deal with the complex and evolving practices of managed health care. It provides information on a number of key managed care issues along with insights into how managed care generally works and some ways to gain and maintain cost-efficient, high-quality health care coverage. Most helpfully, it includes advice from managers on quality management, claims and benefits administration, and managing employee or patient demands. It might not be the Bible of managed care, but the *Handbook* is considered by many to be one of the standard resources for the managed care industry.

Kongstvedt, Peter. *Managed Care: What It Is and How It Works*, 2nd edition. Sudbury, Mass.: Jones and Bartlett Publishers, 2004.

For those who don't have the arm strength to lift the big version or the time to read it, this pocket-sized text provides a concise understanding of managed health care. As you might have guessed, much of its information is taken from its parent text, *The Managed Health Care Handbook,* fourth edition. Perhaps the book's most helpful features are its learning objectives and glossary of key managed health care terms.

Laing, Joann Mills. *The Small Business Guide to HSAs.* New York: Brick Tower Press, 2004.

This is an easy-to-follow book that explains what health savings accounts are and compares them to other health coverage options. It lays out some criteria to help determine if a health savings account might be a good option for a particular business, and it explains how to set up and run one. There is also an informative companion Web site, HSAfinder.com.

Curtis, Rick, Trishz Kurtz, and Larry S. Stepnick, eds. *Creating Consumer Choice in Healthcare.* Chicago: Health Administration Press, 1998.

This collection of essays is most useful for the examples it gives of selecting and using performance information to make health care spending decisions. In particular, it provides some helpful tips on how to format information so that it is more understandable for employees.

Hall, Mark A. *Making Medical Spending Decisions: The Law, Ethics, and Economics of Rationing Mechanisms.* New York: Oxford University Press, 1997.

This text explores the process of making rationing decisions, with specific attention to the influences of politics, ethics, and the law. Its writing style is for policy makers, which might make it less appealing to those looking for specific and concrete guidance or ideas for how to handle particular dilemmas. Still, for those with an interest in ethics, law, and health care rationing, this book provides a terrific description of the legitimate, inevitable limits of health care coverage and the factors that influence how these limits play out.

Daniels, Norman, and James E. Sabin. *Setting Limits Fairly: Can We Learn to Share Medical Resources?* New York: Oxford University Press, 2002.

This book is a cross between health policy and philosophy. A very thoughtful book that was influential in the development of the Ethical Force Program's consensus report on fair coverage decisions, on which the present book was based. Daniels and Sabin compare resource allocation dilemmas across countries as well as within the United States, and they propose a number of universal ethical considerations that they suggest should drive health care spending decisions. Their chapters on pharmacy benefits management and lung volume reduction surgery provide tangible and carefully analyzed examples.

Danis, Marion, Carolyn Clancy, and Larry R. Churchill, eds. *Ethical Dimensions of Health Policy.* New York: Oxford University Press, 2002.

This collection of essays includes some especially relevant pieces on how ethics can influence health policies. It is not directed at employers, or, for that matter, to the dilemma of selecting health benefits. But it gives very lucid explanations of how the ethical concepts we drew on for this book can and should also come into play throughout the health care system.

Ubel, Peter A. *Pricing Life: Why It's Time for Health Care Rationing.* Cambridge, Mass.: MIT Press, 2001.

In this provocative book, in addition to calling for open use of the "R" word in health care, Dr. Ubel discusses some of the options for how to go about rationing health care resources. His exploration of cost-effectiveness analysis is especially helpful, as is his review of studies looking at how Americans think about equity, or fairness.

Organizations, Web Sites, and Newsletters

Agency for Healthcare Research and Quality
http://www.ahrq.gov/

In their own words, "The Agency for Healthcare Research and Quality (AHRQ) is the lead federal agency charged with improving the quality, safety, efficiency, and effectiveness of health care for all Americans. As one of twelve agencies within the Department of Health and Human Services, AHRQ [pronouned "ark"] supports health services research that will improve the quality of health care and promote evidence-based decisionmaking." Serving all segments of the health care system, this Web site is well organized and huge, and it contains innumerable reports and other information and resources that will be helpful for you in making decisions about health care coverage and for your employees as they navigate the health system.

America's Health Insurance Plans
http://www.ahip.org/

This trade organization works on behalf of health plans through lobbying, research, quality assurance, and education. Their Web site provides important insights into the health care industry that can be of great use to employers.

Center for Studying Health System Change
http://www.hschange.com/

The Washington-based Center for Studying Health System Change (HSC) is a nonpartisan policy research organization. HSC designs and conducts studies focused on the U.S. health care system to help policy makers in government and private industry make informed decisions. Its "Community Tracking Surveys" are especially interesting, but the Web site is loaded with useful studies and reports.

Healthfinder
http://www.healthfinder.gov/

Published by the U.S. Department of Health and Human Services, this Web site is very useful for encouraging healthy lifestyles and choices by your employees. It includes a library of information, decision-making help when dealing with various sectors of the health care system, and a thorough list of organizations that may prove helpful for human resources personnel and other employees. It is also available in Spanish.

HealthGrades®
http://www.HealthGrades.com

HealthGrades® is a publicly traded, for-profit healthcare ratings organization. They provide ratings of hospitals and physicians that could be used by employers as they decide among different health plans and employees as they choose specific provider organizations. They also offer an electronic newsletter.

National Business Group on Health
http://www.wbgh.com

Formerly the Washington Business Group on Health (hence the WBGH in their domain name—no, that's not a typo), the NBGH is a nonprofit organization "exclusively devoted to representing the perspective of large employers and providing practical solutions to its members' most important health care problems." The NBGH has recently focused increasingly on "providing business solutions" for its members' health care benefits dilemmas, in addition to its research and advocacy agenda.

National Business Coalition on Health
http://www.nbch.org

The NBCH is a Washington, D.C.–based coalition of coalitions. It is made up of about ninety local and regional business coalitions, with a shared mission of working toward "value-based purchasing of health care services" through concerted employer action to measure quality and provide incentives to improve quality, all of which make up a movement they call "Community Health Reform."

National Committee for Quality Assurance
http://www.ncqa.org

NCQA is an independent, nonprofit organization whose mission is to improve health care quality. They provide a number of reports (including the previously discussed HEDIS® reports) that employers and human resources personnel will find useful when evaluating health plans.

Wellness Program Management Advisor
http://www.healthresourcesonline.com

As this book went to press, the editors of "Wellness Program Management Advisor" had just released a special report, "Monitoring the Effectiveness of America's Worksite Wellness Programs: Containing Healthcare Costs Through the Most Effective Programs, and How You Can Get There, Second Edition." The report is available on their Web site and it compiles the experiences of workplace wellness managers in a variety of settings. It looks like it will be a help to any employer starting or continuing a wellness program; it includes insights and straightforward discussions of the successes and frustrations of wellness managers.

Finally, although we've focused on organizations and resources that work primarily on health care, we'll also briefly mention that there are a number of organizations that we have used as resources on employee benefits more generally, including the following.

American Benefits Council
http://www.americanbenefitscouncil.org/

A membership lobbying organization, the American Benefits Council operates in Washington, D.C., where it aims "to ensure that employers providing health care coverage are protected from undue burdens and provided maximum flexibility. The Council also provides news on pending and recent legislation."

Employee Benefit News
http://www.benefitnews.com/

An online resource for benefits and human resources professionals. Developed and maintained by a full-time staff of business journalists, this Web site delivers information to help benefits decision makers keep current on benefits issues and news and share ideas and solutions with their peers.

Employee Benefit Research Institute
http://www.ebri.org/

In its own words, "The mission of the Employee Benefit Research Institute (EBRI) is to contribute to, to encourage, and to enhance the development of sound employee benefit programs and sound public policy through objective research and education." They offer a wide variety of resources on their Web site, including reports on much of their research, a benefit bibliography, and some educational resources.

International Foundation of Employee Benefit Plans
http://www.IFEBP.org

The International Foundation of Employee Benefit Plans is the largest educational association serving the employee benefits and compensation industry. A nonprofit, nonlobbying organization, we have found the foundation to be a good resource for objective, accurate, and timely information.

Benefits Link
http://benefitslink.com/index.html

In their own words: "Our audience is people who administer, give compliance advice about, design, make policy for, or otherwise are concerned with, employee benefit plans in the United States sponsored by either private or governmental employers."

Index